GUIDE FOR A CHURCH UNDER ISLĀM

GUIDE FOR A CHURCH UNDER ISLĀM

The Sixty-Six Canonical Questions
Attributed to Theodōros Balsamōn

A Translation of the Ecumenical Patriarchate's
Twelfth-Century Guidance to the
Patriarchate of Alexandria

Patrick Demetrios Viscuso
Foreword by Sidney H. Griffith

HOLY CROSS ORTHODOX PRESS
BROOKLINE, MASSACHUSETTS

© 2014 Patrick Viscuso
Published by Holy Cross Orthodox Press
50 Goddard Avenue
Brookline, Massachusetts 02445
ISBN 978-1-935317-46-3

Library of Congress Cataloging-in-Publication Data

Balsamon, Theodore, active 12th century.
    Guide for a church under Islam : the sixty-six canonical questions attributed to Theodoros Balsamon; a translation of the Ecumenical Patriarchate's twelfth-century guidance to the Patriarchate of Alexandria / Patrick Demetrios Viscuso; foreword by Sidney H. Griffith
        pages cm
    In English; translated from Greek.
    Includes bibliographical references.
    ISBN 978-1-935317-46-3
    1. Canon law--Orthodox Eastern Church. 2. Orthodox Eastern Church--Doctrines. I. Viscuso, Patrick, 1956- II. Griffith, Sidney Harrison. III. Title.
    KBS199.6.B35G8 2013
    261.2'7--dc23
                                                                    2013019511

To my wife, Susan,
and my son, Sebastian

CONTENTS

APPENDIXES

FOREWORD

During the long years from the Islāmic conquest of the territories of the Oriental patriarchates in the mid-seventh century until the time in the mid-to-late twelfth century when Theodōros Balsamōn served the Church as Orthodox patriarch of Antioch *in absentia*, little accurate information about the daily lives of the Christians living among the Muslims reached Constantinople or Rome. Refugee monks, local chroniclers, and itinerant churchmen brought reports of expropriations of property and harsh treatment, but not much news about how Christians lived their faith under Muslim rule was recorded in texts that would one day become available to historians. A number of local writers composed apologetic or polemical texts meant to strengthen the faith of Christians faced with the challenge of Islām, and some of these works eventually came to the attention of their co-religionists in the wider Greek- and Latin-speaking world. One readily recalls the work of St. John of Damascus in this connection, but there were many others. For example, the earliest known Christian thinker regularly to write in defense of the Christian faith in Arabic was the sometime monk of Mar Sabas and Orthodox bishop of Harrān, Theodōros Abū Qurrah (ca. 755–ca. 830), a number of whose works were translated into Greek and circulated widely from the ninth century onward. But he and the others after him tell us little about the ecclesiastical life of ordinary church people in the world of Islām.

Even when much of the territory of the patriarchate of Antioch returned to Byzantine rule for a time, beginning in the middle of the tenth century, what little is heard of the daily life of Christians there is fragmentary. And it is against the background of this meager serving of available information about the Christians of the Islāmic world that the treasure trove of Balsamōn's canonical answers to the questions put to him by inquirers living in the patriarchate of Alexandria in the twelfth century comes to our aid. It was an important moment in Egyptian history when in the last years of the century Fāṭimid rule gave way to the Ayyūbid era and Sunnī Islām once more became dominant in Egypt. The change in regime inaugurated a crescendo in Sunnī scholarship that would in due course make Cairo an important center of Islāmic learning. Meanwhile, in the patriarchate of Alexandria a new generation of Arabic-speaking, Coptic Orthodox Christian scholars was emerging, and by the middle of the thirteenth century they were producing a substantial archive of Christian theology and biblical commentary that would soon lead them into interreligious colloquy with leading Muslim thinkers. It was against this background that Orthodox Christians in Alexandria sent their canonical questions to Theodōros Balsamōn, struggling as they were with both the problems of living within an Islāmic polity and the tensions of their relationships with other Christians in the same milieu with whom they were not in communion.

The questions posed to the learned canonist and the answers he returned, few as they are in number, provide a rare glimpse into the daily ecclesiastical life of his co-religionists who looked to Constantinople for guidance in matters large and small, in a time and place where Christian life was difficult. His responses, carefully reasoned and sensitive to local difficulties, not only gave much needed practical advice to the immediate inquirers, but in the long run they also made a valuable contribution to the larger body of Orthodox canonical literature that guides the Church to this day.

Patrick Viscuso's translations of Balsamōn's responses to sixty-six canonical queries from Alexandria to Constantinople offer us much more than just a timely English version of an important canonical text from the Middle Ages. In the introduction to the translation and in the explanatory notes to the text, he provides the reader with an insightful commentary that places the canonical exchange within its historical context both in relation to the ecclesiastical and political developments within the contemporary Byzantine world and in view of current events in the world of Islām, especially those affecting the lives of Christians living among the Muslims. What is more, Viscuso writes in a clear style that does justice to the original Greek of the queries and responses, takes into account earlier scholarship on the work, and renders the text in communicable English that readily conveys both the sense and the significance of Balsamōn's solicitude for those who sought his informed counsel. In the process, the reader also learns much about the Ecumenical Patriarchate's interest in and care for a sister church living in difficult circumstances.

Patrick Viscuso's *Guide for a Church under Islām* makes a welcome contribution not just to the history of canon law, but perhaps more importantly to the history of Christianity under Islām, a much-neglected area of Church history that increases in relevance to modern Church life with every passing day in the early decades of the twenty-first century.

Sidney H. Griffith
The Catholic University of America
Washington, DC

PREFACE

The purpose of this study is to promote the exploration of Orthodoxy's canonical tradition and, ultimately, to promote its appropriation for the needs of the contemporary Church. Through the Church's canonical life, truth is expressed in the circumstances of history to address specific situations, categories of behavior, persons, and institutional structures. In this sense, canon law may be viewed as the Church's ministry in applying its teachings to practical situations in the life of each Christian.

One of the challenges that the Church faces is the fact that within the modern age it has not appropriated its received formal corpus of canon law. In contrast, during the late Byzantine period, there were systematic approaches to translate the canons into a contemporary application.

Perhaps a starting point for our own understanding of the canons and development of a methodology for their study would be a translation of the great commentators of canon law during the twelfth century—Theodōros Balsamōn, Iōannēs Zonaras, and Alexios Aristēnos—all of whom examined the received body of canon law in light of the Church's needs in their own age. Although separated from us by culture, language, and time, their translation into contemporary language could provide insights into approaches and the development of a context for our own examination of the Church's nature as a divine-human reality.

The previously untranslated twelfth-century *Canonical Questions of the Most Holy Patriarch of Alexandria, Lord Markos, and the Answers for them by the Most Holy Patriarch of Antioch, Lord Theodōros Balsamōn* represents a genre of canon law texts known variously as "canonical answers" (κανονικαὶ ἀποκρίσεις), "canonical questions" (ἐρωτήσεις κανονικαί), "questions" (ἐρωτήσεις), "questions and answers" (ἐρωτήματα καὶ ἀποκρίσεις, or ἐρωταποκρίσεις), and "answers" (ἀπαντήσεις), which follow a question and answer format. Such works could be promulgated by a synod or an individual bishop and enjoyed great popularity as an application of formal legislation to practical circumstances. In this sense, these works may be viewed as pastoral manuals or guides usually directed to a clerical audience.

The work under examination contains questions submitted by a church under Islāmic rule and corresponding guidance framed by the Ecumenical Patriarchate through one of its most learned canonical experts. The guidance covers a wide range of issues ranging from marriage to the administration of ecclesiastical finances. What do these questions reveal about the ordering of Church life? Does the historical context restrict the answers to the age in which they were created, or is there a significant meaning that may still be derived? Are there understandings that may assist the Church in its relationship with Islām? The present work is an invitation to further study and exploration.

I express my gratitude to my colleagues, especially the Rev. Dr. Sidney Griffith, Dr. David Olster, Dr. John Birkenmeier, and Dr. Anton Vrame for their support in creating this volume. I would also like to thank the Rev. Fr. Costas Pavlakos, the Rev. Dr. Stephen Zorzos, Dr. Lewis Patsavos, Mr. John Margetis, Mr. Georgios Theodorides, Mrs. Gabriela Fulton, and the faculty of the Antiochian House of Studies for their encouragement and support of my efforts. Furthermore, I wish to acknowledge the generosity of Dr. Margaret Mullet, Director of Byzantine Studies, and Dr. Deborah Brown, Librarian (Dumbarton Oaks Research Library and Collection); the Rev. Dr. Joachim Cotsonis, Director of the Archbishop Iakovos Library and Learning Resource Center (Holy Cross Greek Orthodox School of Theology); and Mr. Paul Finley, former Executive Director, Mr. John Scanlan, present Executive Director (Antiochian Village Heritage and Learning Center), and Ms. Julia Ritter, Curator and Librarian (Antiochian Heritage Museum and Library), for extending the resources of their respective institutions. I wish to express my special thanks to the Rev. Dr. Joseph Allen, whose loyal friendship is a constant assistance.

Most of all, I thank my wife, Susan, and son, Sebastian, who continue to make sacrifices that enable my scholarship.

Finally, I thank His Eminence Archbishop Demetrios of the Greek Orthodox Archdiocese of America for his support of my work. My gratitude is especially heartfelt for the spiritual guidance of His Eminence Metropolitan Philip of blessed memory, late Primate of the Antiochian Orthodox Christian Archdiocese of North America and founder of the Antiochian House of Studies, and His Grace Bishop Thomas, the hierarchical overseer of the Antiochian House of Studies and Bishop of Charleston, Oakland, and the Mid-Atlantic of the Antiochian Archdiocese. I express my gratitude for having been granted the privilege and honor of teaching canon law at the Antiochian House of Studies, where many of hours of research were performed.

Εἰς πολλὰ ἔτη Δέσποτα.

Principal Abbreviations

Angold

Michael Angold, *Church and Society in Byzantium under the Comneni, 1081–1261* (Cambridge: Cambridge University Press, 1995).

Bat Ye'or, *Decline*

Bat Ye'or, *The Decline of Eastern Christianity under Islam: From Jihad to Dhimmitude; Seventh–Twentieth Century* (Madison: Fairleigh Dickinson University Press, 1996).

Beck

Hans-Georg Beck, *Kirche und Theologische Literatur im Byzantinischen Reich* (Munich: C. H. Beck'sche Verlag Buchhandlung, 1959).

Berger

Albrecht Berger, *Das Bad in der Byzantinischen Zeit* (Munich: Institut für Byzantinistik und neugriechische Philologie, 1982).

BMFD

J. Thomas and A. Constantinides Hero, eds., *Byzantine Monastic Foundation Documents: A Complete Translation of the Surviving Founders' Typika and Testaments*, 5 vols., Dumbarton Oaks Studies 35 (Washington, DC: Dumbarton Oaks Research Library and Collection, 2000).

Bosworth	C. E. Bosworth, "The 'Protected Peoples' (Christians and Jews) in Medieval Egypt and Syria," *Bulletin of the John Rylands University Library of Manchester* 62, no. 1 (1979): 11–36.
Brain	Peter Brain, *Galen on Bloodletting: A Study of the Origins, Development and Validity of his Opinions, with a Translation of the Three Works* (Cambridge: Cambridge University Press, 2009).
C. Th.	Codex Theodosianus.
Cameron, *Heresiology*	Averil Cameron, "How to Read Heresiology," *Journal of Medieval and Early Modern Studies* 33, no. 3 (2003): 471–492.
CFHB	*Corpus Fontium Historiae Byzantinae.*
Chon	Nikētas Chōniatēs, Χρονικὴ διήγησις, ed. J. L. van Dieten, in *Nicetae Choniatae historia*, 2 vols., CFHB 11.1–2 (Berlin and New York: Walter de Gruyter, 1975); English translation by Magoulias.
Darrouzès, "Le traité"	Jean Darrouzès, "Le traité des transferts : Édition critique et commentaire," REB 42 (1984): 147–214.
Darrouzès	Idem, *Rescherches sur les ΟΦΦΙΚΙΑ de l'Église Byzantine* (Paris: Institute Français d'Études Byzantines, 1970).
DDC	R. Naz et al., eds., *Dictionnaire de Droit Canonique, contenant tous les termes du droit canonique, avec un sommaire de l'histoire et des institutions et de l'état actuel de la discipline,* 7 vols. (Paris: Letouzey et Ané, 1935–1965).
Dölger	Dölger, Franz. *Regesten der Kaiserurkunden des oströmischen Reiches von 565–1453*: vol. 1, fasc. 1, *Regesten von 565–867*, ed. Andreas E. Müller, 2nd ed. (Munich: C. H. Beck,

2009); vol. 1, fasc. 2, *Regesten von 867–1025*, ed. Andreas E. Müller, 2nd ed. (Munich: C. H. Beck, 2003); vol. 2, *Regesten von 1025–1204*, ed. Peter Wirth, 2nd ed. (Munich: C. H. Beck, 1995); vol. 3, *Regesten von 1204–1282*, ed. Peter Wirth, 2nd ed. (Munich: C. H. Beck, 1977); vol. 4, *Regesten von 1282–1341* (Munich: C. H. Beck, 1960); vol. 5, *Regesten von 1341–1453*, co-authored by Peter Wirth (Munich: C. H. Beck, 1965). (References are to the documents, which are numbered in chronological order consecutively throughout.)

DOP   *Dumbarton Oaks Papers.*

DTC   Alfred Vacant, E. Mangenot, and Emile Amann, eds., *Dictionnaire de Théologie Catholique, contenant l'exposé des doctrines de la théologie catholique, leurs preuves et leur histoire*, 15 vols. in 23 pts. (Paris: Letouzey et Ané, 1903–1950).

Durǎ   Nicolae Durǎ, "The Ecumenicity of the Council in Trullo: Witnesses of the Canonical Tradition in East and West," in Nedungatt, 229–262.

EA   Ἐκκλησιατικὴ Ἀλήθεια.

EB   *Études byzantines.*

EO   *Échos D'Orient.*

Evaggelatou-Notara   Φλωρεντία Ευαγγελάτου-Νοταρά, "Οποῖόν ἐστι μέρος τῆς ἀστρολογίας κακιζόμενόν τε καὶ ἀποτρόπαιον (Αστρολογία-Αστρονομία καὶ οι σχετικές αντιλήψεις κατά τον ΙΒ' αιώνα)," in Oikonomides, 447–463.

Fattal   Antoine Fattal, *Le statut légal des non-musulmans en pays d'Islam* (Beirut: Imprimerie Catholique, 1958).

FBR	*Forschungen zur Byzantinischen Rechtsgeschichte.*
Frend	W. H. C. Frend, *The Rise of the Monophysite Movement: Chapters in the History of the Church in the Fifth and Sixth Centuries* (Cambridge: Cambridge University Press, 1972).
Friedmann	Yohanan Friedmann, *Tolerance and Coercion in Islam: Interfaith Relations in the Muslim Tradition* (Cambridge: Cambridge University Press, 2003).
Gedeōn	Μανουὴλ Γεδεών, "Θεοδώρου Βαλσαμῶνος λύσεων κανονικῶν διάφοροι γραφαί," EA 35 (1915): 169–173, 177–182, 185–189.
Gedeōn, *Nea*	Idem, "Λύσεις ἐπὶ ταῖς ἀπορίαις τοῦ ἁγιωτάτου πατριάρχου Ἀλεξανδρείας κῦρ Μάρκου ἐξενεχθεῖσαι ἐπὶ τῆς πατριαρχίας τοῦ ἁγιωτάτου πατριάρχου Κωνσταντινουπόλεως, κῦρ Γεωργίου τοῦ Ξιφιλίνου," NB 1 (1903): 135–160.
Gray	Patrick T. R. Gray, *The Defense of Chalcedon in the East (451–553)* (Leiden: E. J. Brill, 1979).
Griffith	Sidney H. Griffith, *The Church in the Shadow of the Mosque: Christians and Muslims in the World of Islam* (Princeton: Princeton University Press, 2008).
Griffith, "Melkites"	Idem, "'Melkites,' 'Jacobites,' and the Christological Controversies in Arabic in Third/Ninth Century Syria," in Thomas, 9–56.
Grillmeier	Aloys Grillmeier, *Christ in Christian Tradition*: vol. 1, *From the Apostolic Age to Chalcedon (451)*, trans. John Bowden, 2nd ed. (Louisville, KY: Westminster John Knox Press, 1975); vol. 2, *From the Council of Chalcedon*

(451) to Gregory the Great (590–604),
pt. 1, *Reception and Contradiction: The
Development of the Discussion about
Chalcedon from 451 to the Beginning
of the Reign of Justinian,* trans. John
Cawte and Pauline Allen (Louisville,
KY: Westminster John Knox Press,
1986); vol. 2, pt. 2, *The Church in
Constantinople in the Sixth Century,*
co-authored by Theresia Hainthaler,
trans. John Cawte and Pauline Allen
(Louisville, KY: Westminster John
Knox Press; London: Mowbray, 1995);
vol. 2, pt. 3, *The Churches of Jerusalem
and Antioch,* co-authored by Theresia
Hainthaler, Luise Abramowski, Tanios
Bou Mansour, Andrew Louth, and
Marianne Erhardt (Oxford: Oxford
University Press, 2013, forthcoming);
vol. 2, pt. 4, *The Church of Alexandria
with Nubia and Ethiopia after 451,*
co-authored by Theresia Hainthaler,
trans. O. C. Dean (Louisville, KY:
Westminster John Knox Press; London:
Mowbray, 1996).

Grumel, *La Chronologie*	Venance Grumel, *La Chronologie* (Paris: Presses universitaires de France, 1958).
Grumel, "Περὶ μεταθέσεων"	Idem, "Le Περὶ μεταθέσεων et le patriarche de Constantinople Dosithée," EB 1 (1943): 239–249.
Grumel, "La profession"	Idem, "La profession médicale à Byzance à l'époque des Comnènes," REB 7 (1949): 42–46.
Grumel, "Les réponses"	Idem, "Les réponses canoniques à Marc d'Alexandrie, leur caractère official, leur double redaction," EO 38 (1939): 321–333.
Hall	Stuart George Hall, ed. and trans., *Melito of Sardis, On Pascha and*

	Fragments, Oxford Early Christian Texts (Oxford: Clarendon Press, 1979).
Hartmann	Wilfried Hartmann and Kenneth Pennington, eds., *The History of Byzantine and Eastern Canon Law to 1500* (Washington, DC: The Catholic University of America Press, 2012).
Herbut	Joachim Herbut, *De Ieiunio et Abstinentia in Ecclesia Byzantina* (Rome: Libreria Editrice della Pontificia Università Lateranense, 1969).
Herman	E. Herman, "Balsamon (Théodore)," in DDC, 2:76–83.
Horna	Konstantin Horna, "Die Epigramme des Theodoros Balsamon," *Wiener Studien, Zeitschift für klassiche Philologie* 25 (1903): 165–215.
Izzo	Jaunuarius M. Izzo, *The Antimension in the Liturgical and Canonical Tradition of the Byzantine and Latin Churches* (Rome: Pontificium Athenaeum Antonianum, 1975).
Jeffreys	Elizabeth Jeffreys, John Haldon, and Robin Cormack, eds., *The Oxford Handbook of Byzantine Studies* (Oxford: Oxford University Press, 2008).
Joannou	Périclès-Pierre Joannou, ed., *Discipline générale antique*: vol. 1, pt. 1, *Les canons des conciles oecuméniques (IIe–IXe s.)* (Grottaferrata, Italy: Tipografia Italo-Orientale "S. Nilo," 1962); vol. 1, pt. 2, *Les canons des synodes particuliers (IVe–IXe s.)* (Grottaferrata, Italy: Tipografia Italo-Orientale "S. Nilo," 1962); vol. 2, *Les canons des pères grecs (IVe–IXe s.)* (Grottaferrata, Italy: Tipografia Italo-Orientale "S. Nilo," 1963); vol. 3, *Index* (Grottaferrata, Italy:

Tipografia Italo-Orientale "S. Nilo," 1964).

Johnston
Ian Johnston, *Galen on Diseases and Symptoms* (Cambridge: Cambridge University Press, 2006).

Katsaros
Βασίλης Κατσάρος, Ἰωάννης Κασταμονίτης, Συμβολή στη μελέτη του βίου, του ἔργου και της ἐποχῆς (Θεσσαλονίκη: Κέντρο Βυζαντινῶν Ἐρευνῶν, 1988).

Kazhdan, *Change*
Alexander Kazhdan and Ann Wharton Epstein, *Change in Byzantine Culture in the Eleventh and Twelfth Centuries* (Berkeley, CA: University of California Press, 1985).

Kazhdan, "The Image"
Alexander Kazhdan, "The Image of the Medical Doctor in Byzantine Literature of the Tenth to Twelfth Centuries," DOP 38 (1984): 43–51.

Koukoules
Phaidōn Koukoules, *Βυζαντινῶν βίος και πολιτισμός*, 6 vols. (Athens: Institut Français d'Athènes, 1948–1957).

Krüger
Paul Krüger, ed., *Justinian's Institutes*, trans. Peter Birks and Grant McLeod (Ithaca, NY: Cornell University Press, 1987).

Kühn
C. G. Kühn, ed., *Claudii Galeni Opera Omnia*, 20 vols., 1821–33 (reprint, Hildesheim: Georg Olms, 1964–1965).

Laiou
Angeliki E. Laiou, "God and Mammon: Credit, Trade, Profit and the Canons," in Oikonomides, 261–300.

Laiou, *Consent*
Angeliki E. Laiou, ed., *Consent and Coercion to Sex and Marriage in Ancient and Medieval Societies* (Washington, DC: Dumbarton Oaks Research Library and Collection, 1993).

Laiou, "Sex"   Angeliki E. Laiou, "Sex, Consent, and
                        Coercion in Byzantium," in Laiou,
                        Consent, 109–221.

Laiou and Simon   Angeliki Laiou and Dieter Simon, eds.,
                        Law and Society in Byzantium, Ninth–
                        Twelfth Centuries (Washington, DC:
                        Dumbarton Oaks Research Library and
                        Collection, 1994).

Larin   Vassa Larin, *The Byzantine Hierarchical*
                        Divine Liturgy in Arsenij Suxanov's
                        Proskinitarij (Rome: Pontificio Istituto
                        Orientale, 2010).

Le Coz   Raymond Le Coz, ed. and trans., *Jean*
                        Damascène: Écrits sur l'Islam, Sources
                        Chrétiennes 383 (Paris: Éditions du
                        Cerf, 1992).

Leib   Bernard Leib, ed. and trans., *Anne*
                        Comnène: Alexiade (Règne de
                        l'empereur Alexis I Comnène), 3 vols.
                        (Paris: Belles Lettres, 1937–1945).

Levy-Rubin   Milka Levy-Rubin, *Non-Muslims in the*
                        Early Islamic Empire: From Surrender
                        to Coexistence (Cambridge: Cambridge
                        University Press, 2011).

L'Huillier   Peter L'Huillier, *The Church of the*
                        Ancient Councils: The Disciplinary
                        Work of the First Four Ecumenical
                        Councils (Crestwood, NY: St. Vladimir's
                        Seminary Press, 1996).

Lokin, "Law"   J. H. A. Lokin, "The Significance of Law
                        and Legislation in the Law Books of the
                        Ninth to Eleventh Centuries," in Laiou
                        and Simon, 71–91.

Magdalino, "Constantinople" Paul Magdalino, "Constantinople and
                        the ἔξω χῶραι in the time of Balsamon,"
                        in Oikonomides, 179–197.

Magdalino, *Empire*   Idem, *The Empire of Manuel I*
                        Komnenos, 1143–1180 (Cambridge:
                        Cambridge University Press, 1993).

Magdalino, *L'Orthodoxie*	Idem, *L'Orthodoxie des astrologues: La science entre le dogme et la divination à Byzance (VIIᵉ–XIVᵉ siècle)* (Paris: Lethielleux, 2006).
Macrides	Ruth Macrides, "Nomos and Kanon on Paper and in Court," in Rosemary Morris, ed., *Church and People in Byzantium: Society for the Promotion of Byzantine Studies; Twentieth Spring Symposium of Byzantine Studies, Manchester, 1986* (Birmingham: Centre for Byzantine, Ottoman and Modern Greek Studies, University of Birmingham, 1990).
Magoulias	Harry J. Magoulias, *O City of Byzantium: Annals of Niketas Choniatēs* (Detroit: Wayne State University Press, 1984).
Menevisoglou	Pavlos Menevisoglou, "La signification canonique et ecclésiologique des titres épiscopaux dans l'Église Orthodoxe," *Kanon* 7 (1985): 74–90.
Menevisoglou, *Historical*	Παῦλος Μενεβίσογλου, *Ἱστορική εἰσαγωγή εἰς τούς Κανόνες τῆς Ὀρθόδοξου Ἐκκλησίας* (Στοκχόλμ: Ἡ Ἱερά Μητρόπολις Σουηδίας καὶ πάσης Σκανδιναβίας, 1990).
Menevisoglou, *Myron*	Idem, *Τὸ Ἅγιον Μύρον ἐν τῇ Ὀρθοδόξῳ Ἀνατολικῇ Ἐκκλησίᾳ: ἴδια κατὰ τὰς πηγάς καὶ τὴν πράξιν τῶν νεότερων χρόνων τοῦ Οἰκουμενικοῦ Πατριαρχείου* (Θεσσαλονίκη: Τὸ Πατριαρχικόν Ἵδρυμα Πατερικῶν Μελετῶν, 1972).
Menevisoglou, *Syntagma*	Idem, *Τὸ Σύνταγμα Ράλλη καὶ Ποτλῆ καὶ ἄλλαι ἐκδόσεις ἱερῶν κανόνων κατὰ τὸν 19ον καὶ 20ὸν αἰώνα* (Αθήνα: Ἐκδόσεις Ἐπέκταση, 2009).
Milaš	Nikodim Milaš, *Das Kirchenrecht der morgenländischen Kirche: nach den allgemeinen Kirchenrechtsquellen und*

	nach den in den autokephalen Kirchen geltenden Spezial-Gesetzen, trans. Alexander R. v. Pessić, 5 vols., 2nd ed. (Mostar, Herzegovina: Pacher & Kisić, 1905).
Miller	Em. Miller, "Lettres de Théodore Balsamon," *Annuaire de L'Association pour L'Encouragement des Études Grecques en France* 18 (1884): 8–19.
Mommsen	Theodor Mommsen and Paul Krueger, eds., *The Digest of Justinian*, trans. Alan Watson, 4 vols. (Philadelphia: University of Pennsylvania Press, 1985).
Mortreuil	Jean Anselme Bernard Mortreuil, *Histoire du droit byzantin: ou du droit romain dans l'Empire d'Orient, depuis la mort de Justinien jusqu'à la prise de Constantinople en 1453*, 3 vols. (Paris: E. Guilbert, G. Thorel, 1843–1846).
Muraoka	Takamitsu Muraoka, *A Greek-English Lexicon of the Septuagint* (Walpole, MA: Peeters, 2009).
NB	*Νέα Βιβλιοθήκη Ἐκκλησιαστικῶν Συγγραφέων*.
Nedungatt	George Nedungatt and Michael Featherstone, eds., *The Council in Trullo Revisited* (Rome: Pontificio Istituto Orientale, 1995).
Noailles	P. Noailles and A. Dain, eds. and trans., *Les Novelles de Léon VI le Sage* (Paris: Belles Lettres, 1944).
OCA	*Orientalia Christiana Analecta.*
OCP	*Orientalia Christiana Periodica.*
ODB	A. Kazhdan et al., eds. *The Oxford Dictionary of Byzantium*, 3 vols. (New York and Oxford: Oxford University Press, 1991).

Oikonomides	N. Οἰκονομίδης, ed., *Τὸ Βυζάντιο κατὰ τὸν 12ο αἰώνα: κανονικὸ δίκαιο, κράτος καὶ κοινωνία* (Ἀθήνα: Ἑταιρεία βυζαντινῶν και μεταβυζαντινῶν μελετῶν, 1991).
Papastathis	Charalambos Papastathis, ed., *Byzantine Law: Proceedings of the International Symposium of Jurists, Thessaloniki, 10–13 December 1998* (Thessaloniki: Bar Association of Thessaloniki, 2001).
Petit	L. Petit, "Balsamon, Théodore," in DTC, 2:135–138.
PG	J.-P. Migne, ed., *Patrologiae cursus completus: Series graeca*, 161 vols. in 166 pts. (Paris: 1857–1866).
Pitsakēs	Κωνσταντίνος Πιτσάκης, "Ἡ ἔκταση τῆς ἐξουσίας ἑνὸς ὑπερόριου πατριάρχη: ὁ πατριάρχης Ἀντιοχείας στὴν Κωνσταντινούπολη τὸν 12ο αἰώνα," in Oikonomides, 91–139.
REB	*Revue des études byzantines.*
Reg	*Les Regestes du Patriarcat de Constantinople (Le Patriarcat Byzantine, Série I)*: vol. 1, *Les Actes de Patriarches*, fasc. 1, *Les Regestes de 381 à 715*, by Venance Grumel, ed. Jean Darrouzès, 2nd ed. (Paris: Institut Français d'Études Byzantines, 1972); vol. 1, fasc. 2–3, *Les Regestes de 715 à 1206*, by Venance Grumel, ed. Jean Darrouzès, 2nd ed. (Paris: Institut Français d'Études Byzantines, 1989); vol. 1, fasc. 4, *Les Regestes de 1208 à 1309*, by Vitalien Laurent (Paris: Institut Français d'Études Byzantines, 1971); vol. 1, fasc. 5, *Les Regestes de 1310 à 1376*, by Jean Darrouzès (Paris: Institut Français d'Études Byzantines, 1977); vol. 1, fasc. 6, *Les Regestes de 1377 à 1410*, by Jean Darrouzès (Paris:

Institut Français d'Études Byzantines, 1979); vol. 1, fasc. 7, *Les Regestes de 1410 à 1453*, by Jean Darrouzès (Paris: Institut Français d'Études Byzantines, 1991). (References are to the documents, which are numbered in chronological order consecutively throughout.)

Renoux

Ch. Renoux, "'Les fêtes et les saints de l'Église arménienne' de N. Adontz," *Revue des Études Arméniennes* 14 (1980): 277–305.

Rhallēs and Potlēs

Γ.Α. Ῥάλλης and Μ. Ποτλής, *Σύνταγμα θείων καὶ ἱερῶν Κανόνων τῶν τε Ἁγίων καὶ Πανευφήμων Ἀποστόλων καὶ τῶν ἱερῶν Οἰκουμενικῶν καὶ τοπικῶν Συνόδων καὶ τῶν κατὰ μέρος Ἁγίων Πατέρων*, 6 vols. (Ἀθήνα: Γ. Χαρτοφύλαξ, 1852–1859).

Scheltema, A

H. J. Scheltema and N. van der Wal, eds., *Basilicorum Libri LX: Series A*, 8 vols. (Groningen, Netherlands: J. B. Wolters, 1953–1988).

Scheltema, B

Idem, *Basilicorum Libri LX: Series B*, 9 vols. (Groningen, Netherlands: J. B. Wolters, 1953–1988).

Simonsohn

Uriel I. Simonsohn, *A Common Justice: The Legal Allegiances of Christians and Jews Under Early Islam* (Philadelphia: University of Pennsylvania Press, 2011).

Stevens

Gerardus Petrus Stevens, *De Theodoro Balsamone, Analysis Operum ac Mentis Iuridicae* (Rome: Libreria Editrice della Pontificia Università Lateranense, 1969).

Stolte, "Basilika"

Bernard H. Stolte, "Balsamon and the Basilika," *Subseciva Groningana: Studies in Roman and Byzantine Law* 3 (1988): 115–125.

Stolte, "Nomokanon"	Idem, "In search of the origins of the Nomokanon of the Fourteen Titles," in Papastathis, 183–194.
Tafel	G. L. F. Tafel, *Eustathii metropolitae Thessalonicensis opuscula*, 1832 (reprint, Amsterdam: A. M. Hakkert, 1964).
Taft, "Omophorion"	Robert F. Taft, "The Case of the Missing Vestment: The Byzantine Omophorion Great and Small," *Bolletino della Badia Greca di Grottaferrata* 3, no. 1 (2004): 273–301.
Taft, *Precommunion*	Idem, *A History of the Liturgy of St. John Chrysostom*, vol. 5, *The Precommunion Rites*, OCA 261 (Rome, 2000).
Taft, "Pontifical Liturgy 1, 2"	Idem, "The Pontifical Liturgy of the Great Church According to a Twelfth-Century Diataxis in Codex *British Museum Add. 34060*," OCP 45 (1979): 279–307 and 46 (1980): 89–124.
Taft, "Women"	Idem, "Women at Church in Byzantium: Where, When—and Why?" DOP 52 (1998): 27–87.
Thomas	David Thomas, ed., *Syrian Christians under Islam: The First Thousand Years* (Leiden, Netherlands: Brill, 2001).
Tritton	A. S. Tritton, *The Caliphs and Their Non-Muslim Subjects* (London: Oxford University Press, 1930).
Trōianos	Σπύρος Τρωιάνος, "'Ράλλης καὶ Ποτλής,'" in Oikonomides, 17–24.
Trōianos, "Ἰατρική"	Idem, "Ἰατρική επιστήμη και γιατροί στο ερμηνευτικό έργο των κανονολογών του 12ου αιώνα," in Oikonomides, 465–481.
Viscuso, *Casebook*	Patrick Viscuso, *Orthodox Canon Law: A Casebook for Study*, 2nd ed.

	(Brookline, MA: Holy Cross Orthodox Press, 2011).
Viscuso, "Cleanliness"	Idem, "Cleanliness, Not a Condition for Godliness: *Alousia* as a Canonical Requirement in Late Byzantium," *Greek Orthodox Theological Review* 46, nos. 1–2 (2001): 75–88.
Viscuso, "Death"	Idem, "Death in Late Byzantine Canon Law," *Ostkirchliche Studien* 51 (2002): 225–248.
Viscuso, "Images"	Idem, "Theodore Balsamon's Canonical Images of Women," *Greek, Roman, and Byzantine Studies* 45 (2005): 317–326.
Viscuso, "Marital"	Idem, "Marital Relations in the Theology of the Byzantine Canonist Theodore Balsamon," *Ostkirchliche Studien* 39 (1990): 281–288.
Viscuso, "Nikodemos"	Idem, "The Theology of Marriage in the *Rudder* of Nikodemos the Hagiorite," *Ostkirchliche Studien* 41 (1992): 187–207.
Westerink	L. G. Westerink, ed. and trans., *Nicholas I Patriarch of Constantinople: Miscellaneous Writings* (Washington, DC: Dumbarton Oaks, 1981).
Woodfin	Warren T. Woodfin, *The Embodied Icon: Liturgical Vestments and Sacramental Power in Byzantium* (Oxford: Oxford University Press, 2012).
Zepos	I. Zepos and P. Zepos, eds., *Jus Graecoromanum*: vol. 1, *Novellae et aureae bullae imperatorum post Justinianum*; vol. 2, *Leges imperatorum Isaurorum et Macedonum*; vol. 3, *Theophili Antecessoris Institutiones. Libellus de temporibus ac dilationibus. Tractatus de pecullis. De Actionibus*; vol. 4, *Practica ex actis Eustathii*

Romani. Epitome legume; vol. 5, *Synopsis Basilicorum*; vol. 6, *Ecloga privata aucta. Epanagoge aucta. Ecloga ad pochiron mutata. Synopsis minor*; vol. 7, *Prochiron auctum. Meditattio de nudis pactis Michaelis Pselli synopsis legum. Michaelis Attaliotae opus de jure. XXVI Decisiones Demetrii Chomatiani*; and vol. 8, *Codex civilis moldaviae. Codes civilis Valachiae. Collectio morum Graecorum localium* (Athens: Georgii Fexis, 1931; reprint, Darmstadt: Scientia Aalen, 1962).

PART ONE

INTRODUCTION

This brief essay will present systematically the historical context for the Byzantine legal text under consideration, which is known from its manuscript tradition under the title *Canonical Questions of the Most Holy Patriarch of Alexandria, Lord Markos, and the Answers for Them by the Most Holy Patriarch of Antioch, Lord Theodōros Balsamōn* (Ἐρωτήσεις κανονικαὶ τοῦ ἁγιωτάτου πατριάρχου Ἀλεξανδρείας κυρίου Μάρκου καὶ ἀποκρίσεις ἐπ᾿αὐταῖς τοῦ ἁγιωτάτου πατριάρχου Ἀντιοχείας, κυρίου Θεοδώρου τοῦ Βαλσαμών).[1] This examination will explore questions regarding authorship, canonical nature, dating, Church-state relations, intra-Christian interactions, and Islāmic influence. On the basis of this background, the reader will have a foundation for understanding the translation of the twelfth-century Byzantine work.

The Byzantine Empire and Theodōros Balsamōn

The Byzantine Empire was the medieval Eastern Roman Empire. Its establishment is often dated from the reign of Kōnstantinos the Great (324–337) and the founding of Constantinople as the New Rome and its capital in 330.[2] Especially in its earlier history, the empire domi-

---

1. Rhallēs and Potlēs, 4:447; Reg, 1184. Throughout this study the writing will be referred to as the *Canonical Questions*.

2. There is considerable disagreement on this point. For example, some scholars date the beginning of the Byzantine era with the reign of Theodosios I

nated the Mediterranean and even included parts of present-day Western Europe, much of the Middle East, and North Africa. During the twelfth century, the empire was reduced to territory in the Balkans, parts of the Middle East, and a portion of the Anatolian littoral.

After a period of instability in the eleventh century marked by frequent changes of emperors and severe losses of territory and resources, the first three members of the Komnēnos family established relative stability in imperial rule. These emperors were: Alexios I Komnēnos (r. 1081–1118), Iōannēs II Komnēnos (r. 1118–1143), and Manouēl I Komnēnos (r. 1143–1180). After Manouēl I and until 1204, the empire suffered setbacks under Alexios II Komnēnos (r. 1180–1183), Andronikos I Komnēnos (r. 1183–1185), and Isaakios II Angelos (r. 1185–1195, 1203–1204). During the twelfth century, among the threats to the empire were the Normans, Turks, Pechenegs, Serbs, Hungarians, Armenians, and the armies of Latin crusaders and their states.

The Church's division into an Orthodox East and Latin West is traditionally dated to the mutual excommunications of 1054 promulgated by representatives from the sees of Rome and Constantinople.[3] Prior to its division ecclesiastical governance had become centralized in the churches of Rome, Constantinople, Alexandria, Antioch, and Jerusalem, with its foundations fixed through the legislation of the first four ecumenical councils (Nicea 325, Constantinople 381, Ephesos 431, and Chalcedon 451) that ranked their order of primacy. The patriarch of Constantinople, who held the title of Ecumenical Patriarch, administered the church of the Eastern capital with a synod of metropolitan bishops representing sees from throughout Asia Minor. The pope of Alexandria and his synod had authority over Egypt, which was under Islāmic rule after the Arab invasions of the mid-seventh century.

Theodōros Balsamōn, to whom authorship of the *Canonical Questions* is attributed, lived during the last half of the twelfth century. Balsamōn was probably a native of the Byzantine capital of Constantinople based on a remark made in his commentary on canon 28 of the Fourth Ecumenical Council of Chalcedon (451): "I, who am a pure Constantinopolitan, who became a member of the most holy throne of Constantinople, by the grace of God, most of all, wish and

---

the Great (r. 379–395), Ioustinianos the Great (r. 527–565), or Leōn III the Isaurian (r. 685–741) for various reasons.

3. Modern scholarly opinion is divided on the causes and dating of the split.

pray that Constantinople would have without scandal all the privileges bestowed upon her by the divine canons."[4] He also appears to have belonged to a noble family and was regarded among his contemporaries as having an expert knowledge of law.[5] The placement of Balsamōn's end date after 1195 is determined through the present work, the *Canonical Questions*, since this text is the last attributed to the canonist.

Although the dates of his birth and death are unknown, his career can be traced through sources that either record his actions or make mention of the position titles he held. In documents attributed to him, Balsamōn's titles are deacon of the Great Church of St. Sophia in the capital, *chartophylax*, *nomophylax*, *prōtos* of the Monastery of *Blachernai*, and patriarch of Antioch.[6]

During the reigns of the Komnēnian emperors (1081–1185), the clergy of the Great Church provided many of the episcopal candidates throughout the Byzantine Empire. Their preparation consisted of formal education as well as practical learning through various positions attached to the Church of St. Sophia, particularly in the roles exercised by its deacons. This clergy was also appointed to offices of the patriarchate and court.[7]

The *chartophylax* was considered the "right hand" of the patriarch in his episcopal duties in the capital; he was responsible for drafting canonical documents and even ascertaining the canonicity of proposed marital unions and ordinations. Balsamōn compares the relationship between the *chartophylax* and the patriarch of Constan-

---

4. Rhallēs and Potlēs, 2:285–286.

5. According to the account of the Byzantine historian Nikētas Chōniatēs, a certain Iōsēf Balsamōn was married to the sister of the nobleman Iōannēs Hagiotheodōritēs (Chon, 1:59). Modern scholarship (e.g., Horna, 166; and Stevens, 5) usually assumes that this Balsamōn was a relative of the canonist. Chōniatēs described Theodōros Balsamōn as a "man who was skilled in the law above all others at that time," during the reign of Isaakios II Angelos (r. 1185–1195, 1203–1204) (Chon, 1:406).

6. Such a listing occurs in the case of the *Nomokanōn in 14 Titles* (Rhallēs and Potlēs, 1:31). For an exhaustive treatment of Byzantine ecclesiastical offices, see Darrouzès. In a title given to one of Balsamōn's letters, he was also listed as a *prōtosynkellos* (Miller, 13), an imperial dignity granted by the emperor to metropolitan bishops, derived from the word for "cell" (*synkellos*), and implying a close relationship with the patriarch and the exercise of liaison duties between the Church and imperial court (Angold, 36–38).

7. Angold, 89–98.

tinople as that of Aaron to Moses.[8] The office of *nomophylax* was a civil position involving matters requiring legal expertise in addition to responsibility for training others in the civil law, particularly in the imperial code, or *Basilika*.[9] The position of *prōtos* or *hēgoumenos* was that of abbot over a monastery; in the case of Balsamōn, the monastery was located in the capital and reflected a prestigious appointment.

During the twelfth century, in the crusader Principality of Antioch, a Latin patriarch, Aimery of Limoges (patriarch of Antioch, ca. 1139–ca. 1196), was chosen to head the local church. Balsamōn's appointment before 1190 to the patriarchate of Antioch within the Byzantine Empire was to a position in exile and never involved his physical occupation of the see.[10] As in the case of many of his pre-

---

8. Ibid., 58–59; Darrouzès, 334–353.

9. Beck, 116. The *Basilika* was an imperial code issued under the reign of Emperor Leōn VI (r. 886–912) in sixty books and incorporated the legislative work of the emperor Ioustinianos the Great (r. 527–565). There is a large body of modern scholarship dealing with its legal issues and historical context.

10. The date before 1190 is established based on the account of Nikētas Chōniatēs regarding Balsamōn's assignment by Isaakios II Angelos to write a treatise on the transfer of bishops (Chon, 1:406–407) when the see of Constantinople became vacant in 1189. Balsamōn undertook the work when the emperor gave him the impression that the canonist was the leading candidate for the throne of the capital (Margoulias, 223):

> Having cast out Leontios in this fashion, he decided to contrive the transfer of Dositheos, the patriarch of Jerusalem, and to elevate him to the ecumenical throne. He knew that this was proscribed by the canons and so the deceitful Isaakios summoned Theodōros Balsamōn, the patriarch of the throne of Theoupolis [the city of God], great Antioch, the man most learned at that time in the law. As he conversed with him in private, he pretended to be distressed over the fact that the church should be so lacking in pious and learned men, that monastic virtue should have dissipated and vanished, and that the patriarch no longer shone forth as a daily and ever-moving beacon or skillfully governed the complement of the faithful from the helm of his holy throne. Expressing with indignation these and other such sentiments by a way of a prelude, he led him on, saying that in the past he had wished to remove him from the lampstand of the Antiochians to the patriarchal eminence as a brilliant lamp of the laws shining afar, but that he had refrained from making the transfer because it was forbidden long ago by the canons and was not in accordance with the ecclesiastical ordinances. If he, as an expert in laws and canons, could demonstrate such a precedent in the past, then such a transfer now would be accepted by the majority. The deed would truly be deemed a godsend, and the

decessors to the throne of Antioch, the emperor appointed the patriarch, who was in turn consecrated by the patriarch of Constantinople, a practice firmly established by the ordination of Iōannēs III of Antioch (996–1021). Such an imperial appointment is reflected in the unenforced Treaty of Devol (1108) between Alexios I Komnēnos and the crusader Bohemond I of Antioch (b. ca. 1058 or 1059–d. ca. 1109 or 1111), in which the latter was said to have agreed that the man selected to be patriarch would be from the flock (τῶν θρεμμάτων) of Constantinople and chosen by the emperor.[11]

Nevertheless, the appointment was not to a titular office, in the modern sense of bearing the title of a formerly existing see and acting in complete dependence on the local ordinary.[12] The Byzantines continued to consider Antioch as a territory of the empire and a see of the Church. According to the modern scholar Kōnstantinos Pitsakēs, surviving evidence indicates that the exiled patriarchs of Antioch did not participate in administrative or judicial actions of the Holy Synod of Constantinople as ordinary members. They joined its discussions as visiting hierarchs only in matters of a more general ecclesiastical nature or concerning doctrine.[13] This is consistent with Balsamōn's statement that during the visit of Patriarch Markos of Al-

---

promotion could take place without delay or censure. Thus did the emperor woo Theodōros of Antioch, and the latter assented to this course of actions. After that day, there were gatherings of bishops throughout the patriarchal palace, synods and deliberations concerning transfer. The concession was granted at once and confirmed by imperial decree. The patriarch of Antioch was left patriarch of Antioch, and Dositheos was elevated from the throne of Jerusalem to that of Constantinople.

Modern scholarship no longer identifies a well-known treatise entitled *Concerning transfers* (Περὶ μεταθέσεων) with the work of Balsamōn referenced in the account above (Darrouzès, "Le traité"). Compare the earlier study of the same work by Grumel, "Περὶ μεταθέσεων"; and see Darrouzès, "Le traité," 162–163, n. 29; and Pitsakēs, 108–112, for comments on the latter's conclusions.

11. Leib, 3:134.

12. Menevisoglou, 78–80.

13. For a discussion of the relationship of patriarchates of Constantinople and Antioch during the twelfth century, see Pitsakēs, who provides extensive evidence of the Balsamōn's exercise of patriarchal authority in Constantinople as well as in-depth discussions of whether the Antiochian see was considered canonically vacant during the exile of its patriarchs and whether the monastery of the *Theotokos tōn Hodegōn* was the residence of the patriarchs of Antioch in Constantinople.

exandria, he participated in the Holy Synod's discussions in order to
address general matters of liturgical usage.[14]

Balsamōn exercised his patriarchal authority by issuing canonical documents as patriarch of Antioch, independent of the Holy
Synod of Constantinople. For example, Balsamōn provides canonical instructions on fasting to the "clergy and laity in the throne of
the Great Antioch,"[15] instructions that appear under the title *Letter of
the most holy patriarch of Antioch, Lord Theodōros Balsamōn, concerning the fasting that ought to be practiced each year, which was
sent to the Antiochians.*[16] In addition, the canonist's writings provide
evidence that he exercised hierarchical authority over the hearing
of confessions within his patriarchate.[17] Nevertheless, this does not
diminish the fact that during the time of Balsamōn, the patriarchate
of Antioch functioned as a "satellite" of the Ecumenical Patriarchate
through the appointment and consecration of its clergy.[18]

Throughout the Komnēnian period, the Byzantine emperor
followed the policy of exercising the role of disciplinarian (ἐπιστημονάρχης) of the Church by dominating and controlling the Church's
leadership and resources, but at the same time increasing its institutional strength. Through control and strengthening of the Church
at the same time, the emperor used the Orthodox faith as a unifying
ideology for the empire and exercised control over Byzantine society.[19]

The Komnēnian emperors enlarged this control by promoting
the establishment of canon law and increasing ecclesiastical legislation, particularly in the area of marriage, which determined property relations, family alliances, social position, and other important
aspects of social organization.[20] In this context, as an expert in civil
and canon law, Balsamōn was given an imperial and patriarchal man-

---

14. "The Alexandrians say there is even a divine sacred rite of St. Markos,
which also they use very much. During a synod, and much more also before the
holy emperor, I discussed this when the patriarch of Alexandria stayed in the
capital" (Rhallēs and Potlēs, 2:378).

15. Ibid., 4:421.

16. Ibid., 4:565–579.

17. Ibid., 2:70. Other examples of the exercise of patriarchal authority are
also found in Pitsakēs's study, including epigrams that contain Balsamōn's
reflections on his patriarchate.

18. Pitsakēs, 99.

19. This is the compelling argument advanced by Michael Angold and summarized in Angold, 1–12. The author discusses the meaning of ἐπιστημονάρχης
in Angold, 99–101.

20. Ibid., 103–108, 404–425.

date under Emperor Manouēl I Komnēnos and Ecumenical Patriarch
Michaēl III (1170–1178) to produce commentaries on the *Nomokanōn
in 14 Titles* and the Byzantine church's received corpus of formal canonical legislation belonging to the latter.[21] While often showing the
application of canons to contemporary circumstances, provisions
from the civil law, mainly the *Basilika*, were integrated into his commentaries.[22] As patriarch of Antioch, Balsamōn completed the work
and dedicated his commentaries to Geōrgios II Xiphilinos, patriarch
of Constantinople (1191–1198). This dedication likely symbolized the
work's official recognition and approval by the Ecumenical Patriarchate. Balsamōn is credited with substantial contributions to the
development of Byzantine ecclesiastical law.[23]

Other canonical works, including the authorship of formal decisions of the Holy Synod, are attributed to Balsamōn.[24] Among these
decisions are the Ecumenical Patriarchate's responses to the canonical questions from the Church of Alexandria in 1195.

---

21. An official collection combining canon and civil law, the *Nomokanōn*
was the work of many hands beginning with its anonymous editor in the
seventh century. This editor is often called "Anonymous/Enantiophanēs" based
on his reference in the *Nomokanōn* to a work entitled Περὶ Ἐναντιοφανειῶν
("Concerning Apparent Contradictions") as his own writing (*Nomokanōn* 4.10,
in Rhallēs and Potlēs, 1:124). The *Nomokanōn* came to be attributed to Phōtios
the Great, patriarch of Constantinople (858–867, 877–886), during whose
reign it was revised. The jurist Theodōros Bestēs reworked the text ca. 1090
into the edition that Balsamōn eventually used for his commentary. In this
edition the *Nomokanōn* contains summaries of law and references to canons
organized by subject under fourteen titles, which in turn are divided into
chapters. The attached received corpus of formal canonical legislation includes
the apostolic canons, canons of the ecumenical and local councils, and patristic
texts regarded as having canonical authority. Balsamōn states that the immediate cause for his commentary was due to confusion over whether prior imperial
legislation not included in the *Basilika*, legislation that would have allowed
Patriarch Michaēl III's appointment of a bishop to the see of Amisos, remained
valid (Rhallēs and Potlēs, 1:31–33). See Beck, 146; Lokin, "Law"; Macrides;
Hartmann, 138–141; Stolte, "Basilika"; and Stolte, "Nomokanon" for additional
discussion.

22. For an overview of Balsamōn's treatment of the *Basilika* in his commentaries, see Stolte, "Basilika."

23. Angold, 8.

24. A list of attributed works is contained in Herman, 79–80; Petit,
135–138; and Stevens, 23–128; see Miller for a study of Balsamōn's letters and
Horna for the canonist's epigrams.

The Role of Balsamōn and the Canonical Questions

The introduction to the text of the *Canonical Questions*, which appears to have been written by Geōrgios II Xiphilinos, states that Markos III, patriarch of Alexandria (1180–1209), requested that the Holy Synod of Constantinople address questions generating controversy within the Alexandrian patriarchate. Geōrgios II writes that "because there was internal strife over many ecclesiastical questions," the patriarch of Alexandria, "setting forth a query in writing, . . . entrusted (ἐνεχείρησε) this to Our Mediocrity" (to the patriarch of Constantinople) and "sought that the canonical questions and problems contained in it be discussed in common [namely, in a synod] and that this book of fraternal response be written." An excerpt from Markos's letter follows:

> In the name of the Father, and the Son, and the Holy Spirit. Questions which the Christians dwelling in the land of the Saracens and their possessions ask, which were posed by Markos of Alexandria, the most humble among patriarchs, in the days of our most pious and beloved of Christ emperor Lord Isaakios Angelos, and during the reign of the most holy and ecumenical patriarch Lord Geōrgios, whose years may God increase in length of days. In the month of February of the thirteenth indiction, 1,203 years after the incarnation of our Lord and God and Savior Jesus Christ.

Although not explicitly named as such, the addressees of Markos's letter are most likely Geōrgios II and Isaakios II Angelos. Based on the introduction and excerpt from the patriarchal letter, one can reasonably conclude that Markos's motivation was to have these questions discussed by the Holy Synod of Constantinople and to receive a book (κωδίκιον) with formal responses. The Alexandrian patriarchate was attempting to resolve a number of canonical and liturgical problems arising in a church under Islāmic rule and to harmonize its practices with those of the Great Church of Constantinople. The questions and their associated responses are thus an official document issued by the Holy Synod of Constantinople in response to a series of formal inquiries made between the patriarchates.[25]

---

25. For an excellent discussion of the official nature of the *Canonical Questions*, see Katsaros, 332–334; Grumel, "Les réponses," 321–324; and Reg, 1184. Katsaros's analysis of the introduction and letter provide valuable insights reflected in the discussion above.

Despite the traditional title given to the work, *Canonical Questions of the Most Holy Patriarch of Alexandria, Lord Markos, and the Answers for Them by the Most Holy Patriarch of Antioch, Lord Theodōros Balsamōn*, the patriarchate of Antioch did not have an ecclesial role in this exchange. Balsamōn's participation and contribution in framing answers may be seen as that of a subject matter expert in canonical and legal affairs serving the Ecumenical Patriarchate, whose Holy Synod was ultimately responsible for the decisions underlying the canonical responses. This is reflected in the answers when terms such as "we decided" or "we voted" are used. The role of legal expert was a familiar one to Balsamōn. As seen in the account cited above regarding his composition of a treatise on the transfer of bishops, Balsamōn was employed as a legal expert, but was not in an ecclesial role. Similarly, although authored by Balsamōn, the responses were not an official act of the patriarchate of Antioch, but rather wholly represented the answers of the Ecumenical Patriarchate.[26]

In this way, the "book of fraternal response" is the product of the Holy Synod's deliberations and thus is appropriately preceded by an introduction written by its president, Patriarch Geōrgios II Xiphilinos. The later authority of the *Canonical Questions* is reflected by their inclusion in manuscripts of canonical sources and the modern reference of G. A. Rhallēs and M. Potlēs, which is regarded as an authoritative canonical collection in the Orthodox Church, especially within the Ecumenical Patriarchate and the Church of Greece.[27]

---

26. A comparison between texts of his canonical commentaries with the responses obviously demonstrates their authorship by Balsamōn. Pitsakēs also makes a distinction between Balsamōn's employment as a legal expert in Constantinople and his ecclesial role. Based on an analysis of the canonist's work *Decision regarding the question that was discussed in a synod, concerning whether it is possible for one and the same man to be joined to two second cousins* (Rhallēs and Potlēs, 4:556–564), Pitsakēs concludes that this writing does not reflect Balsamōn's participation in the Holy Synod's discussions as a member of the see of Constantinople, but only of his employment due to his expertise in the law (Pitsakēs, 117). For a discussion of marital theology in the latter work, see Viscuso, "Marital."

27. For an excellent discussion concerning the work of Rhallēs and Potlēs, see Trōianos; and Menevisoglou, *Syntagma*. The latter addresses the question of authorization and endorsement by the Ecumenical Patriarchate (Menevisoglou, *Syntagma*, 21–25). In modern Orthodox canonical collections, the *Canonical Questions* are regarded as representative of a genre of canon law texts known variously as "canonical answers" (κανονικαὶ ἀποκρίσεις), "canonical ques-

The date of February 1203 is problematic since it was in the sixth, not the thirteenth, indiction. At the same time, in that year Geōrgios II Xiphilinos was already dead and Isaakios II Angelos was still dethroned. The modern scholar Konstantin Horna believes that the reckoning of 1,203 years after Christ's birth reflects an eight-year differential between the Byzantine calculation of the world's creation and Western dating, and thus the date should be 1195, which would be in the thirteenth indiction. In February 1195 both Geōrgios II and Isaakios II were still on their respective thrones. Isaakios II would not be overthrown and blinded until April 1195.[28]

---

tions" (ἐρωτήσεις κανονικαί), "questions" (ἐρωτήσεις), "questions and answers" (ἐρωτήματα καὶ ἀποκρίσεις, or ἐρωταποκρίσεις), and "answers" (ἀπαντήσεις), which follow a question and answer format. Such works could be promulgated by a synod or an individual bishop and enjoyed great popularity as an application of formal legislation to practical circumstances. In this sense, these works may be viewed as pastoral manuals or guides usually directed to a clerical audience. The fourth and fifth volumes of Rhallēs and Potlēs contain the standard modern Orthodox collection of this genre. The modern Orthodox canonist Nikodim Milaš views their origin as derived from the practice of official opinions (ius publice respondendi) in Roman civil law (Milaš, 55–56; Hartmann, 168–169, 198–203). The Canonical Questions are the only set of ἀποκρίσεις between the patriarchates of Alexandria and Constantinople published in modern canonical collections. Further manuscript study will be necessary to determine the application of this work in the life of the Alexandrian patriarchate and whether there were additional exchanges.

28. Horna, 169. Horna states that the use of anno Domini dates is rare in Byzantine sources, which generally calculate years based on the creation of the world and indiction number. After the end of the tenth century in Byzantium, creation was generally calculated as occurring 5,509 years before the incarnation. Year one would be equivalent to September 1, 5509 BC through August 31, 5508 BC. In order to convert a date based on modern reckoning to a year according to this Byzantine system, 5,509 would be added from September 1 to December 31 and 5,508 from January 1 to August 31. Horna states that unlike the Byzantine calculation, year dating in Western usage is premised on a world creation date of 5,500 years before the incarnation. Consequently, in order for 1,203 years after the incarnation to be converted to common modern reckoning, eight additional years would need to be subtracted, with the result of 1,195. Horna's argument based on a difference in creation dates is plausible. The modern legal historian J. A. B. Mortreuil makes a similar argument (Mortreuil, 3:453). Whether or not there was a uniform acceptance of 5,500 years in the West, it appears that a conversion to a date based on an eight-year differential makes more sense than other explanations, such as those of Allatius and Beveridge, who appear to attribute the 1203 dating to a copyist mistake (Horna, 169). In addition, the closest years otherwise in a thirteenth indiction would be 1180 or 1210 (or with the addition of eight years, 1188 or 1218),

There is evidence from Balsamōn's commentary on canon 32 of the Council in Trullo that Patriarch Markos III visited the capital and may have been present for a possible 1195 meeting of the Holy Synod:

> Note from the present canon that first of all St. Iakōvos the Brother of God, as the one who was the first hierarch of the Church of Jerusalem, handed down the divine sacred rite, which is unknown among us and is used among the Jerusalemites and Palestinians during great feasts. The Alexandrians say there is even a divine sacred rite of St. Markos, which also they use very much. During a synod, and much more also before the holy emperor, I discussed this when the Patriarch of Alexandria stayed in the capital. For when he was about to celebrate liturgy with us and the Ecumenical Patriarch (οἰκουμενικοῦ) in the Great Church, he began to hold in his hand the liturgical book (κοντάκιον) of the Liturgy of Iakōvos, but was prohibited by him (αὐτοῦ),[29] and consented to celebrate liturgy (ὑπέσχετο λειτουργεῖν) just as also us.[30]

The edition of Rhallēs and Potlēs also presents a variant text:

> Note that from the present canon 32 it appears that the divine sacred service was also handed down from St. Iakōvos the Brother of God, who was the first hierarch of the Church of Jerusalem, which presently neither is found nor known among us, as it is disused. How the clergy in Palestine celebrate liturgy with the mystagogy (μυσταγωγίας) that was handed down, as they say, from the same brother of God, and the bishops in Alexandria and the priests perform sacred services with prayers, as they say, that were handed down by St. Markos, and do not follow what is being done by the clergy throughout the empire (οἰκουμένην), that is to say, they do not pay attention to the mystagogies (μυσταγωγιῶν) handed down from St. Basileios and St. Iōannēs Chrysostomos, I do not know. This was discussed by me both in the synod and much more also at the imperial court (βασιλικοῦ

---

both of which are impossible. For a general discussion of chronology in Byzantium and problems posed by dating, see ODB, 1:342–343, 448–449. More specialized treatment of the world era and dating may be found in Grumel, *La Chronologie*, especially 124–128 regarding the Byzantine era and 257–258 for a table showing indiction years. Venance Grumel also accepts the February 1195 date (Reg, 1184).

29. Patriarch Geōrgios II Xiphilinos.
30. Rhallēs and Potlēs, 2:377–378.

βήματος) when the patriarch of Alexandria was staying in the capital, and when he was about to concelebrate with us, he wished to celebrate with the sacred rite handed down, as he said, from St. Markos, even if he was corrected not by deposition, for which everything seemed sufficient [in this way], but only by the patriarch telling him to no longer do this.[31]

In both accounts of the visit to the capital, it is noteworthy that the Ecumenical Patriarch was considered the authority responsible for addressing any problems arising from the conduct of Markos III. Balsamōn did not view himself as exercising an ecclesial role as a patriarch of Antioch in matters dealing with liturgical and canonical relations between the other two great sees, but the accounts portray his role as that of legal expert when participating in the synodal and imperial discussions within the capital.[32]

In addition to visiting the capital, it is possible that the patriarch of Alexandria may have also personally delivered his letter and questions. Geōrgios II states in the introduction that Markos III, "setting forth a query in writing, . . . entrusted (ἐνεχείρησε) this to Our Mediocrity." The verb "ἐγχειρέω" might also be translated as "to place into one's hands" and could mean that the written inquiry was entrusted during a personal meeting.[33] The first canonical question of the "book of fraternal response" regarding the Liturgies of St. Markos and St. Iakōvos may have also have been a contemporary reflection of the controversy reported during the visit of Markos III and evidence that the synodal discussions took place at the same time.

---

31. Ibid. The editors state that the variant text is present in the "codex of Trebizond." According to Spyros Trōianos, the codex is a manuscript dated 1779, currently catalogued as National Library of Greece 1372, and was copied from another dated 1318 and believed to be Istanbul Serail 115 (see Trōianos, 20).

32. Patriarch Markos III's attempted use of a liturgy (whether that of St. Iakōvos or St. Markos) different from that being used by other celebrants took place in the cathedral church of the Ecumenical Patriarchate. The patriarch of Constantinople would be fully within his prerogatives to enforce consistency of usage during a celebration in the Church of St. Sophia, especially in the basic question of which liturgical text should be used.

33. Grumel, "Les réponses," 330.

Muslims and Non-Muslims in Medieval Egypt

With the Muslim conquest of Egypt by the mid-seventh century, Christians, Jews, and certain other non-Muslims eventually became categorized in accordance with the Qur'ān as "people of the book" or "scriptuaries" (*ahl al-kitāb*), infidels (*kuffār*) who did not convert to Islām but who were recognized as possessing written scriptures and who had entered into a protected relationship with the Muslim state (*dhimma*), notwithstanding that these scriptures were viewed as changed and distorted versions of a divine revelation perfectly expressed in the Qur'ān.[34]

---

34. In classical Islāmic legal sources, Jewish scriptures were often called *Tawrāt*, and the Christian scriptures *Injīl*. These scriptures were divinely revealed books when received by the prophets of Judaism and Christianity, but were subjected to corruption (*taḥrīf*) by later adherents to such an extent that they no longer reflect the divine will when they differ from the Qur'ān (Friedmann, 20). In his treatment of Qur'ānic exegesis, *ḥadīth*, and Islāmic jurisprudence during the first centuries of Islām, Yohanan Friedmann describes the categorizations of unbelievers (Friedmann, 54–55):

> In various contexts, all these are subsumed under the more general categories of infidels (*kuffār*, sg. *kāfir*), scriptuaries (*ahl al-kitāb*), the "protected people" (*ahl al-dhimma* or *dhimmīs*) and the inhabitants of areas under infidel rule (*ahl al-ḥarb* or *ḥarbīs*). In some sources we also have the larger category of "the people who have an agreement" with Muslims (*ahl al-ʿahd*). These are divided into *dhimmīs* (*ahl al-dhimma*), "people of the armistice" (*ahl al-hudna*) and "people who received guarantee of safety" (*ahl al-amān*). The people of the armistice live outside the Muslim territory, are not ruled by Muslims and their only obligation is to refrain from waging war against the Muslims. The people who received guarantee of safety (*mustaʾminūn*) are those who stay in the Muslim area temporarily, do not settle and are not obliged to pay *jizya*. These may be envoys, merchants, seekers of refuge and visitors. *Ahl al-dhimma*, *ahl al-ʿahd* and *ahl al-ḥarb* are concepts defining the relationship between these groups and Muslims in terms of Islamic law; the rest of the terms define the groups in question in terms of religious beliefs. There is some overlapping between these categories: the scriptuaries who live under Muslim rule are at the same time infidels and *dhimmīs*: they agreed to live under Islamic rule and received permanent protection from the Muslims. The scriptuaries who live beyond the frontiers of *dār al-islām* are infidels but not *dhimmīs*: since they have not been awarded the protection of the Muslim community, they are *ḥarbīs*, or *ahl al-hudna*. Jews and Christians are considered scriptuaries, though there is some discussion of the question whether polytheistic elements entered into their systems of belief.

While living as "protected people" (*ahl al-dhimma* or *dhimmīs*) under Muslim rule, the "people of the book" were obliged to pay a poll tax (*al-jizyah*) based on the Qur'ānic text "Fight those among the 'people of the book' who do not believe in Allah and the Last Day, who do not forbid what Allah and His Messenger have forbidden and do not profess the true religion, till they pay the poll tax (*al-jizyah*) out of the hand and submissively" (9:29).[35] While the tax was viewed as compensation for their protection and retention of religion, this did not imply freedom of worship.[36] As a discriminatory tax levied on unbelievers, *al-jizyah* was also a means of inflicting humiliation for their obstinate adherence to false beliefs and failure to embrace Islām.[37]

Their status and treatment as *dhimmīs* was based in the early history of Islām and developed with the increase of conquests and contact with non-Muslim populations. In this regard, there are certain documents that have a special significance, which are known under the title of the *Shurūṭ ʿUmar*; they are traditionally attributed to the second caliph, ʿUmar I ibn al-Khaṭṭāb (r. 634–644), and are considered to be a covenant established with the *dhimmīs*. Modern scholarship does not accept such an attribution. The various ver-

---

35. Cited by Griffith, 15.

36. For an insightful discussion of the difference between retaining religion and freedom of its practice, see Friedmann, 1–12.

37. Friedmann summarizes this point based on his survey of classical Islāmic legal literature (Friedmann, 34):

> Since the early stages of their history, Muslims have come to believe earnestly that Islam was the only true religion. It is the (or, perhaps, *the*) religion in the eyes of God who made it complete and gave it His approval. It is therefore only natural that those who embraced it are superior to those who did not. The Muslims possess positive characteristics: they believe in Allah as the only, omnipotent God, who has no partner; they recognize the crucial role of Muḥammad, the Seal of the Prophets, in the spiritual history of mankind; they observe the commandments promulgated in the Qur'ān, behave according to the prophetic *sunna* and abide by the moral precepts of Islām. The infidels, on the other hand, deny the divine message, obstinately adhere to false beliefs and are steeped in moral depravity. In contradistinction to the verse that we have quoted when describing the Prophet's overtures to non-Muslims in the early Medinese period, the Qur'ān now adopts a harsh tone. It now becomes only natural that humiliation should be inflicted on the People of the Book as a punishment for their obduracy.

sions of the *Shurūṭ 'Umar* are viewed as later developments reflecting practices regarding non-Muslims, agreements that were negotiated with subjugated cities, significant discussions among Muslim jurists, and legal borrowings as well as ideological models adopted from the conquered.[38]

Early individual surrender agreements, which often provided liberal conditions for conquered non-Muslims, were sufficient for an initial period when Muslims were engaged in active conquests and were adjusting to their new roles and familiarizing themselves with their territories. With the consolidation of their conquests, new living conditions developed that brought Muslims into closer proximity with non-Muslim populations.[39] These new circumstances resulted in the perceived need for a consistent canonical approach regarding the status of *dhimmī*s, especially because the formerly agreed-upon liberal conditions that were often contained in a body of contradictory and varying documents infringed on Muslim self-views of their own superiority to nonbelievers, particularly "where public space was involved."[40]

While the *Shurūṭ 'Umar* represented this approach and reached its "classical form" in the ninth century, even prior to this period Muslim rulers began applying codes of rules that mirrored most of its regulations.[41] Its provisions reflected the social disabilities and prohibitions that came to govern those who paid the poll tax. The *Shurūṭ 'Umar* allowed Christians to retain their religion but forbade the construction of new churches, convents, and monasteries as well as the repair of such buildings. It required the involuntary extension of hospitality to Muslim travelers, forbade the teaching of the Qur'ān

---

38. A considerable division of modern opinion exists regarding the *Shurūṭ 'Umar*. Levy-Rubin summarizes current scholarship.

39. Milka Levy-Rubin summarizes this new development (Levy-Rubin, 58; cf. 121–125):

> The Muslims, who were at first mostly conquerors on the move, were now settling down; although in some cases they established their own settlements and cities, the most prominent of which were the *amṣār* such as Kūfa and Baṣra, they often settled in existing towns and cities, thus creating close proximity between the Muslim conquerors and the non-Muslim conquered inhabitants. Moreover, non-Muslims soon settled even in the newly founded Muslim settlements, bringing about a situation in which Muslims and non-Muslims were coexisting side by side.

40. Ibid., 165.

41. Ibid., 100; Griffith, 15.

to non-Muslim children, prohibited public preaching of Christianity
or proselytizing, prevented Christians from obstructing the conversion of their co-religionists to Islām, mandated that Christians rise
as a show of respect and yield their seats when Muslims wished to sit,
forbade non-Muslims to call upon Muslim homes, directed that non-
Muslims not resemble Muslims in dress (specifying that the parting
of the hair and the turban were part of Muslim appearance), prohibited non-Muslims the use of saddles or carrying of swords, forbade
the engraving of Arabic inscriptions on their seals, prohibited their
keeping of pigs in the vicinity of Muslims or the selling of fermented
drinks in general, required non-Muslims to clip their front hair, made
obligatory that non-Muslims dress distinctively from Muslims (particularly wearing a belt known as the *zunnār*), banned public display
of Christian symbols such as the cross, proscribed processions for
either Palm or Easter Sunday, barred the loud use of wooden clappers
(*nawāqīs*) to announce Christian services, separated the location of
non-Muslim from Muslim graves, restricted ownership of slaves from
those allotted to Muslims, and required that non-Muslim houses be
built lower than those of Muslims.[42]

The bulk of these restrictions expressed a new social order with
roots in pre-Islāmic Sasanian ideology that divided society into
hierarchical classes with no mobility between them and placed
non-Muslims as its lowest caste.[43] The adoption of such an ideol-

---

42. A translation of a version of the *Shurūṭ ʿUmar* can be found in Levy-
Rubin, 171–172; cf. Tritton, 5–17; and Fattal, 60–69. Levy-Rubin provides an
in-depth analysis of clauses relating to public space (Levy-Rubin, 145–162)
and demonstrates their roots in the social ideology prevailing in pre-Islāmic
Sasanian society before the conquest.

43. Levy-Rubin provides the following excellent analysis (Levy-Rubin,
167–168):

> Thus, ancient Persian symbols of status and sovereignty such as
> elements of dress and paraphernalia, riding-beasts and riding gear,
> hairstyle, titles, respectable seats, and any other manifestations of
> authority and status were forbidden to the non-Muslims, and were
> appropriated exclusively by the Muslims. Non-Muslims, in contrast,
> had to wear distinctive clothes which suited their inferior position
> in society; just as in Sasanian society the lower class had to dress in
> a manner reflecting their low social station. The concept of *ghiyār*
> or "distinguishing marks" was in fact an established principle in
> Persian society, where "a visible and general distinction" had to be
> made between men of noble birth and common people with regard
> to horses, clothes, ornaments, houses and garden, women and ser-
> vants, drinking-places, sitting- and standing-places. The Muslims

ogy was founded on the Muslims' view of themselves as a "chosen people," their view that "as a result of the gift of Islam the followers of Muḥammad were exalted to this superior position in the world, while the others were to be deprived of the bounties and advantages that they had previously possessed, and were to be degraded and humiliated."[44]

In general, medieval Muslim rule in Egypt afforded a degree of toleration to the "people of the book" due to the special services that they provided, such as being administrators for the Muslim regime and physicians, and practicing professions forbidden to Muslims (e.g., as moneychangers, wine producers, and tanners).[45] The caliphs, or Muslim rulers of the Shīʿī Fāṭimid dynasty (909–1171) in Egypt, made great use of non-Muslims in their regime's bureaucracies. The Sunnī Ayyūbid dynasty (1171–1252), which replaced the Fāṭimids, continued to employ non-Muslims, although those Christians in communion with the Ecumenical Patriarchate, "with their allegiance to a Patriarch in Constantinople . . . were most likely to suffer when there were fears in Egypt of Crusader descents on the coasts."[46]

---

had therefore adopted concepts, values, and status symbols from Sasanian society, and used them as a means of establishing their own superiority. *Shurūṭ ʿUmar* thus reflects the completion of a process in which Muslim society was redefining itself versus the conquered societies. In this new order, Muslims took the place of the upper classes in Sasanian society—the priests, the warriors, and the scribes—while the non-Muslims were allotted the place of the lowest caste in society: the peasants.

44. Ibid., 168.

45. Bosworth, 18. As Levy-Rubin observes, the prohibition on employing *dhimmī*s in government service was not mentioned in the *Shurūṭ ʿUmar* and was difficult to enforce not only because of their irreplaceable expertise in the area of administration and management, but due "probably also to the reluctance of these rulers to replace these loyal and efficient officials who, in contrast to their Muslim counterparts, posed no threat to their rule" (Levy-Rubin, 108).

46. Bosworth, 26. The Sunnī ʿAbbāsid Empire (750–1258), which covered much of the present-day Middle East, had its capital at Baghdad and, for a limited time, at Samarra. The caliphs of the Shīʿī Fāṭimid dynasty who initially ruled in the western area of North Africa expanded into the territory of present-day Egypt in 969 and were rivals to the ʿAbbāsid caliphs. The Ayyūbid dynasty that overthrew them in 1171 acknowledged the suzerainty of the ʿAbbāsid caliphate.

Nevertheless, considerable discrimination was exercised in Muslim law based on the "motif of Muslim exaltedness."[47] This discrimination included the implementation of regulations that mirrored the provisions of the *Shurūṭ ʿUmar* as well as other restrictions such as the principle that non-Muslim testimony was not admissible against Muslims, the denial of the privilege of riding horses by *dhimmīs* "because of the height and respectability of these animals," the requirement for wearing distinctively colored clothing, and the denial of marriage between unbelievers and Muslim women, although the reverse was acceptable in the case of chaste Christian females and Muslim men.[48]

The issuance of such restrictions by al-Mutawakkil (r. 847–861), the tenth caliph of the ʿAbbāsid dynasty, represented a turning point in enforcement of the *Shurūṭ ʿUmar* because "the regulations published by him were to become the norm which the caliphs and other rulers within their orbit strove to impose and enforce."[49] This generalization should be qualified since enforcement of restrictions varied. Nevertheless, although at times disregarded or evaded, the regulations based on the *Shurūṭ ʿUmar* were never annulled and "became the rule in the lands controlled by the caliphs in al-Shām, in Iraq and in Egypt and its dependencies."[50]

---

47. Friedmann, 35.
48. Ibid., 35–37, 160–193; Levy-Rubin, 103–104.
49. Levy-Rubin, 110.
50. Levy-Rubin summarizes this point (ibid., 111):

    However, although enforcement of the *ghiyār* thus seems to have been more significant than has been traditionally assumed, this does not mean that from al-Mutawakkil's days onwards these regulations were an integral and non-negotiable part of *dhimmī* life. It is quite understandable that *dhimmīs* felt more restricted and humiliated than they had before, and that they fought against their new situations, testing and trying the determination of each ruler to enforce the restrictions now and again. It may also be presumed that some rulers were indeed more lenient than others, especially when it suited their internal or external political ends. There are ample examples of allowances and concessions concerning the building of prayer-houses, the employment of *dhimmīs* in government bureaux etc. after al-Mutawakkil's days. Nevertheless, though the rules were often enough disregarded and evaded, they were never annulled and could be imposed or enforced strictly at any moment . . . The evidence thus shows that from al-Mutawakkil's time onwards these regulations became the rule in the lands controlled by the caliphs in al-Shām, in Iraq and in Egypt and its dependencies.

According to C. E. Bosworth, during the medieval period in Egypt "under the stigma of worldly subjugation to another faith, inevitably viewed by many as a manifestation of divine displeasure, and cut off from ready access to sources of spiritual and cultural inspiration like Byzantium and Rome, standards of ecclesiastical discipline and clerical literacy amongst the Eastern Christian churches inevitably declined."[51] Sidney Griffith succinctly states, "These circumstances of necessity put *dhimmī* groups such as Christian communities at risk; in spite of their numbers they became sociological minorities, subaltern populations subject to discrimination, disability, and at times even persecution."[52]

The Christian Communities of Medieval Egypt

The major Christian communities under Muslim rule in Egypt included the Jacobites, Copts, Armenians, Nestorians, Melkites, and Monothelites. When referring to these communities, the *Canonical Questions'* use of expressions such as "Nestorians" did not simply refer to followers living during the time of Nestorios, bishop of Constantinople (428–431). Rather, these terms were "heresy categories" that referred to followers in the sense of those who thought similarly and were used to apply the canonical tradition of the Church to contemporary circumstances. Such categories provided a means of naming, differentiating, and classifying heresies. In so doing, heretics and heresies, such as "Monothelite," "Jacobite," "Armenian," and "Nestorian," were placed in a taxonomy and described according to their nature.[53]

The term "Jacobite" was derived from the name of Jacob Baradaios (Gk. Βαραδαῖος, Syr. Burdʿoyo), the sixth-century missionary and bishop of Edessa (542–578) who rejected the Christological teachings of the Fourth Ecumenical Council of Chalcedon (451) and adhered to those of Sebēros, patriarch of Antioch (512–518). The term was used in the *Canonical Questions* to identify those who thought similarly and did not accept the Fourth Ecumenical Council.

---

51. Bosworth, 19.

52. Griffith, 17; in fact, there were outbreaks of severe persecution, including razing of churches, forced conversions, arrests, confiscations of property (including churches and monasteries), killings, and, most notably, the caliph al-Ḥākim's destruction of the Church of the Holy Resurrection in 1009.

53. For approaches on reading similar documents, see Averil Cameron, *Heresiology*.

Regarding those who rejected Chalcedon, Balsamōn considered the teachings attributed to Eutychēs, archimandrite of Constantinople (b. ca. 370–d. after 451); Dioskoros, pope of Alexandria (444–451); and Sebēros to be identical[54] and offered the following explanation in his introduction to the Fourth Ecumenical Council:

> The Fourth Holy and Ecumenical Council took place in the time of the Emperor Markianos, when 630 holy fathers gathered in Chalcedon against Dioskoros, the renowned ruler over Alexandria, and Eutychēs, archimandrite of Constantinople, who while confessing our Lord Jesus Christ to be consubstantial with the Father, blasphemed concerning the incarnation, and fell into another evil diametrically opposite when fleeing the division of Nestorios, who introduced two sons. For they impiously taught that the two natures of divinity and humanity were commingled after the union and were made into one nature, so also to attribute the passions to the divinity. But they said the Lord did not assume flesh consubstantial with us, composed from the Virgin's blood, but in some unspoken and more divine manner they imagined him to be incarnate, and spoke foolishly of other things. The holy council defrocked and anathematized them while teaching that our Lord Jesus Christ is perfect man and perfect God, undivided and unconfused in two natures. It set forth the canons that follow.[55]

Griffith provides the following summary regarding the consequent development of the "Jacobite" community:

> When the emperor Justinian's policies subsequently forced public allegiance in Byzantium to the Chalcedonian Christological formula, those who followed the faith articulated by the long-deposed Patriarch Severus went underground. Their numbers and their perseverance were increased in the Syriac-speaking communities with the consecration of the sympathetic bishop Jacob Baradaeus (ca. 500–578), who was installed in Edessa in 542 at the behest of the leaders of the Ghassanid Arab tribal confederation who were important allies of Byzantine power on the Syrian and Arabian borders. Subsequently, due to the tireless clandestine activities of Bishop Jacob to support those who rejected Chalcedon and accepted the doctrine of the Patriarchs Cyril of Alexandria

54. Rhallēs and Potlēs, 2:531–532.
55. Ibid., 2:216.

and Severus of Antioch, the whole community of them in the Syriac-speaking milieu came to be called Jacobites by their adversaries.[56]

Griffith states that the community did not "consolidate their denominational identity with their own fully independent hierarchical structures" until after the Islāmic conquests of the seventh century.[57]

The Copts, the dominant Christian community in Egypt during the twelfth century, were "often put together with the Jacobites in discussions of denominational differences."[58] In the *Canonical Questions* this appears also to be the case since there was no separate term used to differentiate them. Nevertheless, although sharing a common faith with Syriac-speaking Jacobites, the Copts preserved a separate communal and ecclesial identity in Egypt, and "had their own early Christian heritage both in their own language, Coptic, and in Greek, the dominant language of learning in the ancient patriarchate of Alexandria and the language in which St. Cyril of Alexandria, the principal theological authority for the Copts, wrote his letters and treatises."[59] However, from the tenth century on, the Copts adopted Arabic, like other Christian communities living under Islām.[60]

In the *Canonical Questions*, although also rejecting Chalcedon, the Armenians were treated as a separate heresy. Regarding the Armenian community under Islām, Griffith summarizes,

> The Armenians too, for the most part, have professed the same faith as the Jacobites while retaining their own independent hierarchical structures and their own language and ecclesiastical literature and cultural traditions. They have borrowed much from Syriac sources, but they have never adopted Arabic as a church language although they have lived in all parts of the Islamic world since the very beginnings of Islam and have long been fluent in Arabic for the purposes of everyday life. Also from the very beginnings of Islam there has been an important Armenian enclave in Jerusalem where they have persistently represented the Jacobite point of view in theological controversies . . . Interestingly, there

---

56. Griffith, 134–135. There is large body of scholarship regarding Christian communities that rejected the teachings of Chalcedon; especially noteworthy are the classic studies of Frend, Gray, and Grillmeier.

57. Griffith, 135.

58. Ibid., 137.

59. Ibid., 136.

60. Ibid.

is even some evidence that from the seventh century onward
there was a group of Armenian Chalcedonians in Jerusalem
engaged in theological activity and producing texts that had
a considerable influence on ecclesiastical and political developments back home in Armenia.[61]

The term "Nestorian" was derived from the name of Nestorios,
bishop of Constantinople (428–431). According to Balsamōn, "Those
who like Nestorios separate God the *Logos* and the humanity assumed by him are called Nestorians."[62] Balsamōn provided the following introduction to the Third Ecumenical Council (431) and ex-
plained Nestorios's theological views:

> The Third Holy and Ecumenical Council took place under
> the reign of the emperor Theodosios the Younger, when two
> hundred fathers gathered in Ephesos, against Nestorios, pa-
> triarch of Constantinople, who said that Christ was a mere
> man, and taught that the Son of God was united with him
> by relationship. For which reason he dared to call the holy
> virgin not Theotokos, but Christotokos. He was defrocked
> and anathematized by the holy fathers.[63]

According to Griffith, "the sociohistorical community lamentably misnamed Nestorian by their adversaries for polemical reasons had its origins not in Patriarch Nestorius's struggles with Patriarch Cyril in Byzantium, but in the Syriac-speaking, academic
communities of Edessa and Nisibis in the days of the schoolman
Narsai (d. 503) and Bishop Bar Sauma of Nisibis (d. before 496)."[64]
These scholars of Edessa and Nisibis generated enthusiasm for
Theodōros of Mopsuestia, Diodōros of Tarsos, and Nestorios, who
came to dominate the theological viewpoints of those who entered
into "communion with the Church of the East, whose patriarchal
see was Seleucia/Ctesiphon in Persia."[65] By the sixth and seventh

---

61. Ibid., 137.

62. Rhallēs and Potlēs, 2:532.

63. Ibid., 2:192.

64. Griffith, 131.

65. Ibid. The Fifth Ecumenical Council (553) condemned the writings of
Theodōros, bishop of Mopsuestia (392–ca. 428), and Diodōros, bishop of Tarsos (378–d. ca. 394), as Nestorian. Emperor Ioustinianos I (527–565) convoked
the council as means of reconciling those rejecting Chalcedon by condemning
theological writings regarded as Nestorian and disassociating the Church from
such views. For a discussion of Ioustinianos's aims, see Gray, 70.

centuries, this community had developed its canonical and ecclesial identity. Extensive theological works were produced in the succeeding centuries in Arabic and Syriac. The Church of the East engaged in extensive missionary work into Southern Arabia, Iran, China, and Southern India.

In the *Canonical Questions* Markos III did not characterize himself as the "Melkite" patriarch of Alexandria, but simply as "patriarch of Alexandria," and his church as "Orthodox." Nevertheless, the fact that his community's theological opponents were described as "Nestorians," "Jacobites," and "Monothelites" marks his church as one that defended the Chalcedonian faith formulated by the Sixth Ecumenical Council (680–681), a position that became associated with the word "Melkite."

"Melkite" (Μελχῖται) was a term derived from the Syriac word *malkāyê* (equivalent in Arabic, *malakiyya*), meaning "imperial" or "royal." Although originally used as an expression of derision by Jacobite and Nestorian theological opponents beginning in the late eighth century at the earliest, the name became connected with the Christian communities of Alexandria, Antioch, and Jerusalem that remained in communion with Constantinople.[66] Their opponents appear to have labeled them as "imperialists" and "royalists" because of their acceptance of councils in which the Byzantine emperors supposedly played an inappropriate role, particularly the Fourth, Fifth, and Sixth Ecumenical Councils, which addressed Christological issues. They professed the faith as taught by these councils and were anti-Jacobite and anti-Monothelite in theology.[67]

In the *Canonical Questions* Monothelitism was portrayed as a heresy that taught that Christ had a single will, a Christological teaching that was condemned by the Sixth Ecumenical Council. In his commentary on the council, Balsamōn provided the following description:

> The Sixth Council took place in this Queen of Cities when Kōnstantinos Pōgōnatos,[68] father of Ioustinianos[69] and a descendant of Herakleios,[70] reigned as emperor. One hundred

---

66. See the discussion above on the use of such terms as "Jacobite" and "Nestorian."

67. Griffith provides a valuable and groundbreaking study of Melkite identity (Griffith, "Melkites").

68. Kōnstantinos IV, emperor (668–685).

69. Ioustinianos II, emperor (685–695, 705–711).

70. Herakleios, emperor (610–641).

seventy holy fathers assembled against Theodōros, who
was a bishop in Pharan; Honorius of Rome; Kyros of Alexandria; Sergios, Pyrrhos, Paulos, and Petros, who presided
in the Church of Constantinople; Makarios of Antioch;
Stephanos his disciple; and Polychronios, an elder of child-
ish mind, who dared to teach that our Lord Jesus Christ has
one will and one energy after the incarnation. They, along
with those who thought the same, were excommunicated
from the Church and anathematized by this holy council,
which taught and confirmed that our Lord Jesus Christ has
two natural wills and two likewise energies after the incarnation, not in a division of persons, but that not one nature
of the two natures of Christ was unwilling or unenergetic,
so that the characteristic properties of each nature are not
done away with (I speak of energy and will), and the two
natures, of which they are characteristic properties, do not
appear combined. [71]

In seeking reconciliation with those who rejected the Christological teachings of Fourth Ecumenical Council of Chalcedon, the
Byzantine emperor Herakleios proclaimed Monothelite teachings in
an *Ekthesis*, or "statement of faith," of 638. The *Canonical Questions'*
use of the term "Monothelite" does not refer to followers living during the time of Sergios I, patriarch of Constantinople (610–638), or
Pyrrhos, patriarch of Constantinople (638–641, 654), who were associated with the seventh-century heresy. As stated above, it was a
"heresy category" that referred to followers in the sense of those who
thought similarly and was used to apply the canonical tradition of
the Church to contemporary circumstances.

The contemporary twelfth-century identity of the "Monothelites"
is not precisely clear from the responses of the *Canonical Questions*.
It can be speculated that the subjects were Maronites, members of
a Syriac-speaking community prominent in the area of Syria/Pales-
tine, which scholarly opinion believes held Monothelite doctrines
and represented a split among Christians adhering to the teachings
of Chalcedon:[72]

In the East this controversy involved an internal split between Greek and Syriac-speaking Chalcedonians them-

---

71. Rhallēs and Potlēs, 2:293–294.
72. For a general overview, see Griffith, 139–140. It should be noted that in
1182 Rome accepted a "Maronite" church into its communion.

selves, into "Monothelete" and "Dyothelete" factions. That there were a significant number of Syriac-speaking "Monotheletes" in Syria in the first/seventh and second/eighth centuries is now abundantly clear from a number of Syriac texts published in recent years by Sebastian Brock. It appears that in so-called "Monothelete" texts, "Dyotheletes" might be called "Maximianists," while "Monotheletes" are sometimes called "Maronites" in both "Jacobite" and "Melkite" texts.[73]

In any case, the use of the term "Monothelite" in the *Canonical Questions* reflected a contemporary division of Chalcedonians between Dyothelite and Monothelite.

As a Dyothelite Chalcedonian, Markos III thus represented a "Melkite" community whose religious identity was defined under Muslim rule and who belonged to the world of Islām in culture and language rather than to Byzantium. The intellectual center for the Melkite community "found throughout the Arabic-speaking world, from Alexandria in Egypt to Antioch in Syria and even in Baghdad," was "the see of Jerusalem and the monasteries of the Judean desert, particularly Mar Sabas."[74]

Their principal theological figure was St. Iōannēs of Damaskos (b. ca. 676–d. 749), also known as Manṣūr ibn Sarjūn, who lived his entire life among Muslims, "albeit all of his surviving writings are in Greek, the theological and liturgical language of the burgeoning Melkite Christian community, whose chief spokesperson he was to become."[75] His writings reflected the identity of the Melkite community formed through its relations with Nestorians, Jacobites, Monothelites, and Muslims in the context of Islāmic culture and society.[76] Although retaining some use of Greek, the Melkite community's adoption of Arabic as a church language took place from the second half of the eighth century onward, and the production of Christian Arabic texts occurred "largely in the monasteries of Jerusalem, the Sinai, and the Judean desert of Palestine."[77]

---

73. Griffith, "Melkites," 13. The word "Maximianist" refers to St. Maximos the Confessor (b. ca. 580–d. 662), who fought against Monotheletism.

74. Griffith, 138.

75. Ibid., 41.

76. See the in-depth discussion of his work in Griffith, "Melkites."

77. Griffith, 49–50.

Concerns and Guidance for a Church under Islām

In the brief analysis that follows, the intention is not to exhaustively comment on each of the responses, but instead to emphasize main themes in the *Canonical Questions* that reflect the concerns of the religious leadership of the Melkite Christian community that lived in the Arabic-speaking world of Islām in Egypt. These observations should be regarded as an invitation to further investigation.

The *Canonical Questions* is the only set of ἀποκρίσεις between the patriarchates of Alexandria and Constantinople published in modern canonical collections. Further manuscript study will be necessary to determine the application of this work in the life of the Alexandrian patriarchate and whether there were additional exchanges.

The subject matter of the questions may be categorized in the following manner:[78]

Liturgy	1, 3, 6, 10, 11, 12, 13, 14, 15, 16, 17, 18, 19, 20, 25, 40, 45, 49, 50, 57, 58, 60
Clergy	9, 21, 22, 24, 26, 27, 28, 29, 31, 33, 34, 38, 39, 40, 42, 43, 59, 61, 62, 63, 66
Communion	10, 11, 12, 13, 15, 16, 17, 18, 19, 20, 36, 45, 52, 60
Matrimony	7, 8, 36, 39, 44, 46, 47, 51, 52, 57, 62, 64, 65
Fasting	12, 51, 52, 53, 54, 55, 56
Heretics	15, 16, 28, 32, 34, 35, 36
Women	7, 8, 37, 38, 50, 65, 66
Sexuality	10, 11, 48, 49, 51, 52
Monasticism	22, 23, 30, 37
Islām	36, 49, 60
Scripture	2
Legal Code	4
Usury	5
Burial	41
Slavery	48

---

78. This categorization scheme is adapted from Stevens, 120, with changed categories, an adjustment of numbering to the Rhallēs and Potlēs edition, and the incorporation of Questions 3, 20, and 21.

By addressing itself to Constantinople, the patriarchate of Alexandria clearly indicated its desire to bring Melkite practices into conformity with those of Ecumenical Patriarchate, especially in the most distinctive and publicly noticeable area, liturgical usages. In seeking to adopt such usages, the Melkite patriarchate may have also been attempting to strengthen its legitimacy in representing the Catholic faith and thereby distinguish itself from the other Christian communities discussed above, which were considered heretical. The *Canonical Questions* reflects concerns on the part of both patriarchates that the central liturgies used for worship were acceptable, services were celebrated in proper locations, celebrations took place at proper times, clergy exhibited a correct appearance in the types of vestments worn, sacred vessels were suitably consecrated, fasting took place at prescribed times (to include abstinence from certain foods, and where applicable, marital relations), and existing indigenous customs were legitimate (such as anointing deceased clergy and burial in churches). In this context, the usages of Great Church were regarded as free from heresy as well as from the effects of Islāmic or crusader domination, and thus a guide or model for other patriarchates.

The response to Question 1 especially emphasizes the need to follow the traditions of the Ecumenical Patriarchate: "All the churches of God ought to follow the custom of New Rome, that is, Constantinople, and to celebrate according to the traditions of the great teachers and luminaries of piety St. Iōannēs Chrysostomos and St. Basileios." Regarding other liturgies, namely, those of St. Iakōvos and St. Markos, "The Catholic Church of the most holy and ecumenical throne of Constantinople does not at all recognize these." The synopsis of *Basilika* 2.1.41 in the response significantly changes the meaning of the law in question. When there is a lack of applicable written law, the synopsis omits the following of local ancient custom and usage, namely, of Alexandria, in favor of the custom of Rome, which is equated with the custom of Constantinople, the New Rome.[79]

---

79. The synopsis reads, "Concerning cases where there is no written law, one ought to observe the custom that Rome has used." Compare the text of *Basilika* 2.1.41, Scheltema, A1:19, which reads, "Concerning cases where a written law does not apply, one must observe custom and usage. And if this is deficient, one must follow what is proximate and similar to what is required. If also neither these things are found, then one must observe the custom that Rome has used. Old usage is observed in place of law. Just as the setting forth

The fact that the Islāmic regimes in Egypt permitted *dhimmī* communities to govern their members according to their own laws when not in conflict with Islām[80] may underlie Question 4 concerning the *Basilika*, the imperial code issued in Byzantium after the Arab conquest: "The sixty books of laws, the so-called *Basilika*, were not issued in our lands, for which reason we do not know their contents. Therefore, we seek to learn whether we are consequently condemned." The response appears to acknowledge Islāmic practice, but at the same time makes allowance for the difficulties of communities living under Muslim rule: "Those boasting of an Orthodox life, whether they might be from the East, or from Alexandria, or elsewhere, are called Romans, and must be governed according to laws, but are not bound by the law that states, 'A Roman man must not be ignorant of law.'"[81]

Based on the statement in the question that "we do not know their contents," the leadership of the Melkite church was obviously not familiar with the imperial code of the Byzantine Empire. The fact that the question was asked raises the issue of legal pluralism and invites exploration of whether the religious leadership of the Melkite church was attempting to find in the imperial code an instrument to enforce the exclusivity of their authority. An examination of this question should consider judicial alternatives that may have been offered by the Islāmic legal system and other Christian communities.[82]

A number of questions deal with the provisions of canon law and canonical opinion regarding marriage and ordination, during a period when such issues were thoroughly discussed, studied, and addressed through synodal decisions within the Byzantine Empire. The fact that the Alexandrian patriarchate was unable to independently resolve such issues may reflect, as Bosworth states, that it was "cut off from ready access to sources of spiritual and cultural inspiration like Byzantium and Rome," and consequently "the standards of ecclesiastical discipline and clerical literacy . . . inexorably declined."[83]

---

of law either is written or unwritten, so also its abolition either takes place through written law, or through the unwritten, that is to say, through disuse."

80. For this practice in medieval Egypt, see Bosworth.

81. This appears to be a maxim based on *Basilika* 2.4.21 (Scheltema, A1:71; cf. *Code* 1.18.12). The phrase "from the East" may be a reference to Balsamōn's own patriarchate of Antioch.

82. As an example of this type of research, see Simonsohn.

83. Bosworth, 19.

The decline of discipline and literacy is exemplified in Question 64, "If a rural priest might perform a benediction of a third marriage, while knowing that it was a third marriage, may he be punished, or as a peasant (χωρίτης) will he be deemed worthy of pardon?" In the response is first stated the principle that "the one ignorant of the fact, whoever he may be, is worthy of pardon in accordance with the laws. The one who is ignorant of the law is not pardoned." This is reinforced with the statement "We say that the priest who had performed a benediction of such an impeded third marriage is to be defrocked, because he was ignorant of the law's main points." Nevertheless, in apparent contradiction, allowance is then made for a lowering of standards: "However, peasants, who are ignorant of the law's fine points, are pardoned sometimes, since legal matters are not clear to all men." The use of the word "peasants" (χωρῖται) and its association with lack of literacy is similar to the response to Question 4, where the point is made that "those who live outside of Rome, namely, peasants (ἀγρόται) and the rest, much more Alexandrians, who do not know the civil law, are pardoned."

Relations with other Christian groups considered heretical are reflected in Question 15:

> Shall one perform priestly rites or pray together without danger with heretics, namely, Jacobites and Nestorians, in their churches or even our own, or might share a common table with them, or perform sponsorship at holy baptism, or perform memorial services of the departed, or commune of the Divine Sanctified Elements with them? For the area's difficulties create many such things, and I seek what one must do.

The "area's difficulties" included not just the existence of such diverse groups ranging from Latins to Monothelites, but that the Jacobites or Copts constituted the majority of Christians. The response emphasizes the Melkites' need to maintain a life separate from other Christian communities:

> Indeed, on this account, we decided that both clergy and laity are subject not only to excommunication and defrocking when they pray together in a church of Orthodox or heretics or whenever they pray together as clergy, or even share a meal together, but also they shall be punished in a more severe way, according to the provisions of the cited divine

canons. For the difficulties of areas, and the increase of heretics, did not change the soundness of the Orthodox faith.

The question, which makes no separation between public ("share a meal together") and religious life, appears to imply that concelebrating services, sharing religious space, and intercommunal relations on a local level are taking place among the Christian communities in Egypt. If true, one of the underlying motivations for the patriarchate of Alexandria's submission of such a question to Constantinople may have been to obtain its support for exclusivity based on the legitimacy and authority of the Melkite patriarchate in distinction to other communities infected with heresy. In this connection, the use of the *Canonical Questions* as a possible guide for lower clergy and local bishops might be explored through a survey of surviving manuscripts containing canonical texts in order to determine the work's dissemination.

The identification of the Catholic Church with the patriarchates of Constantinople, Alexandria, Antioch, and Jerusalem is especially apparent in Question 16 and its response:

> Latin prisoners[84] and others are present in our Catholic churches and seek to partake of the Divine Sanctified Elements. We seek to learn whether this must indeed be permitted.

Response

> The Holy Gospel stated, "He who is not with me is against me, and he who does not gather with me scatters."[85] Therefore, since many years ago the formerly renowned assembly of the Western church (we speak of Rome) separated from the spiritual communion of the other four holy patriarchs, and things alien to the customs and dogmas of the Catholic Church and the Orthodox were excluded, for this reason, the pope is not deemed worthy of the general commemoration of names in the holy sacred rites. A member of the Latin nation ought not be sanctified by a priestly hand through the holy and undefiled Mysteries, unless he first promises to

---

84. At the end of the eleventh century, crusader armies invaded the East. The Battle of Ḥaṭṭīn (1187) resulted in a critical crusader defeat by forces under the leadership of al-Nāṣir Ṣalāḥ al-Dīn Yūsuf ibn Ayyūb (1169–1193), the founder of the Ayyūbid dynasty in Egypt. The prisoners discussed were most likely crusaders captured during this period.

85. Matt 12:30.

refrain from Latin dogmas and customs, is instructed in the
canons, and is made equal to the Orthodox.

The main assumption of this response is that the Catholic
Church consists of the communion of the four ancient patriarchates
(Constantinople, Alexandria, Antioch, and Jerusalem), has holy and
undefiled mysteries, and is Orthodox in faith. Latins are those who
are part of the Western church under Rome, do not share in the communion of the Catholic Church, and have customs and dogmas alien
to the Catholic Church. In light of these assumptions, the central
problem raised by the question is whether Communion should be
given to non-Catholics. The response provides reasons and conditions for barring from the Eucharist and conditions under which
Westerners might receive Communion. They cannot receive while
remaining Latins. Once they are made equal to the Orthodox, that
is, they become Catholic, they can receive the Eucharist. While it is
clear that Westerners must refrain from Latin dogmas and customs
and be instructed in the canons in order to become Orthodox, the
method by which they are received is not specified, that is, whether
by baptism, anointing with *myron*,[86] or confession of faith.

Often cited as an example of Balsamōn's personal intolerance,
perhaps this question and its response should be placed in the context of an affirmation of the Melkite community's self-identity as the
Catholic Church in distinction to others considered heretical, and as
the formal response of the Holy Synod of the Ecumenical Patriarchate in modeling that identity, rather than as the personal opinion
of its legal advisor.[87] At the same time, the affirmation of this self-
identity as the Catholic Church in distinction to others may also be

---

86. The oil of anointing employed for the sacrament or mystery of holy
chrismation following holy baptism, the reception of converts as well as apostates, the consecration of holy altars, the deposit of holy relics, and other uses.
For a survey of canonical literature and discussion of liturgical practice, see
Menevisoglou, *Myron*.

87. For an example of such a view, see Angold, 507–508:

His hostile stance towards the Latins predates his promotion,
but it seems to have become more virulent thereafter. Some of his
more intolerant opinions about the Latins are to be found in the answers he gave around 1195 to a series of inquires by Mark, orthodox
patriarch of Alexandria . . . Not for nothing has Sir Steven Runci-
man singled out Balsamon as the "villain on the Orthodox side for
the development of the schism."

Horna repeats similar sentiments (Horna, 169–170):

linked to a possible need to reinforce the exclusive authority of the
Melkite patriarchate's leadership.

The subject of Question 32 is the manner of reception of converts
from other Christian communities: "Should those who come through
recognition of the truth to the Orthodox faith, namely, Nestorians,
Armenians, Jacobites, and other heretics, be made perfect by holy
myron alone or also by divine baptism?" After citing the provisions
of canon 95 of the Council in Trullo that "it is necessary for Nestorians, Eutychians, and Sebērians to provide written statements and to
anathematize their heresy, also Nestorios,[88] Eutychēs,[89] Dioskoros,[90]
and Sebēros,[91] and the other exarchs of such heresies, those thinking
their things and all the aforementioned heresies, and in this way they
partake of Holy Communion," the conclusion is reached that "in any
event, according to the text of such a canon, some of the heretics are
sanctified by baptism, and others perfected only by holy *myron*."

The ordination of former heretics is the subject of Question 34:

> If the wife and children of a man who came to the faith of the
> Orthodox from heresy, or even others related and sharing
> the same household with him, will not become Orthodox,
> but cling to the former heresy, shall the man perfected, as
> has been stated, through baptism, not be prohibited from
> ascending to priestly or episcopal rank? Or shall he also be
> deprived of such good on account of their evil?

While ordination of those Orthodox "from birth" who married heretics is made dependent on the conversion of their household since
they separated themselves from the assembly and combined "the sinful lot with the portion of Christ," the response makes an exception
for those newly entering the Melkite community:

> If a man who was a member of a heresy from birth might
> choose the Orthodox faith, he shall rightly be deemed wor-
> thy of priestly ordination (if he is not impeded for any other
> reason). The great apostle states, "For how do you know

Wir wissen nicht, ob er die Eroberung Konstantinopels durch
die Kreuzfahrer (1204) noch erlebt hat. Möglich ist es immerhin,
dass er selbst noch die Folgen des Hasses, den er so eifrig gepredigt
hatte, sehen musste.

88. Nestorios, bishop of Constantinople (428–431).
89. Eutychēs, archimandrite of Constantinople (b. ca. 370–d. after 451).
90. Dioskoros, pope of Alexandria (444–451).
91. Sebēros, patriarch of Antioch (512–518).

whether the faithful husband might lead his unbelieving wife to the faith?"[92] Therefore, the man who comes to the Orthodox faith from a heretical sect shall rightly be deemed worthy of priestly rank consistent with the canons, even if his wife and children do not become Orthodox.

The recognition of ordination in other Christian communities is addressed in Question 33: "If a heretical priest or deacon might be deemed worthy of divine and holy baptism, or of sanctification by holy *myron*, shall he serve as a priest with his prior ordination, or might he be deemed worthy of another ordination if he wishes to serve as a priest?" The response cites canon 80 of the holy apostles as determining "that those who came to the Orthodox faith from the pagan life and were baptized are deemed worthy of episcopal rank." The response then asserts, "The former priesthood is considered an abominable ministry and reckoned as not having taken place." Nevertheless, apparently based on the view that the former heresy was not considered worse than paganism, the position is taken that if "blameless regarding his former life," he "might not only be deemed worthy of priestly, but even of episcopal rank" and be consecrated as such "after ascending completely through the customary ranks."

Despite such views of heresy, the Melkite adoption of usages from other Christian communities may be reflected in several questions, for example, those concerning the roles of women and the marriage of clergy: Question 37, "Some women who preside over female monasteries seek episcopal permission on account of hearing the confessions of the nuns under them. Therefore, we seek whether it is possible for this to take place"; Question 38, "The divine canons have made mention of deaconesses. Therefore, we seek to learn what is their ministry"; and Question 39, "Are deacons and subdeacons able to be legally united with wives, or not?" Concerning Eucharistic usages, Question 19 appears to allude to celebrating the Eucharist without the addition of hot water, similar to Armenian practice: "Is it without danger for the administration and reception of the Divine Sanctified Elements to take place with cold wine and water? Or is it necessary also for hot water to be placed into the Holy Things at the time of reception?" In each case, the response emphasizes the need to follow the canonical practice of Constantinople, for example, in regard to the permissibility of marriage after the subdiaconate and

---

92. 1 Cor 7:16 (a paraphrase).

diaconate in Question 39: "Let the one who does this be defrocked, for it was possible for him to do before ordination what was so wickedly dared after ordination." The fact that such questions were asked invites a comparative examination of contemporary Coptic, Jacobite, Armenian, or even Melkite canonical texts.

The existence of Armenian and Syriac speakers who accepted the Christological teachings of the Fourth Ecumenical Council of Chalcedon (451), unlike the majority of their respective communities, may be reflected in Question 6, "Is it without danger for Orthodox Syrians and those from Armenia, but indeed also faithful from other lands, to celebrate in their own language, or are they in every way forced to celebrate with the Greek language?" Griffith mentions the activity of Chalcedonian Armenians in Jerusalem from the seventh century onward and the Syriac Maronite community that entered into communion with the Church of Rome in 1182.[93] In its response, the Ecumenical Patriarchate affirmed, "Those who are Orthodox in all things, even if they might be wholly bereft of Greek speech, will celebrate in their own language with precise copies of the customary holy prayers translated from liturgical books." This answer raises interesting possibilities for further research into the changing identities of the populations that belonged to the Melkite patriarchates under Islām.

Relations with Islām are reflected in questions concerning marriage. Islāmic prohibitions on the intermarriage of Muslim women with Christian husbands were consistent with the canon law of the Melkite community before the Islāmic conquest, since the Church prohibited unions with unbaptized spouses.

On the other hand, the *Canonical Questions* reveals that "marriages" between Christian women and Muslims took place: "Orthodox women are apparently joined in marriage (συνάπτονται τάχα γαμικῶς) with Saracens or even with heretics and wish, like Orthodox as they assert, to partake of the Divine Sanctified Elements. Therefore, we seek what to do."[94] Although called "marriage," these unions were not those formed through the Church or recognized under Byzantine law. The response prohibits the subsequent communion of the Christian wife and requires that such a union end before the woman can be restored to church life: "Indeed how would she be deemed worthy of the Divine Sanctified Elements, when she is cast

---

93. Griffith, 137, 140.
94. Question 36.

out and excommunicated on account of this unlawful communion with a heretic? Absolutely not, unless she might cease from the evil, and be corrected through canonical penances."[95]

On the other hand, the unions of Christian men with Muslim women are not described at all as marriages in Question 49: "If an Orthodox might commit fornication with a Jewish or Hagarene[96] woman, might he be corrected through penance, or shall he be rebaptized?"

The disparity in the descriptions may reflect the influence of Islāmic law. According to its practice, Christian men and Muslim women were not permitted to marry, and any such unions would be considered fornication. Nevertheless, Muslim men could marry Christian women, and the *dhimmī* wife did not have to adopt the Muslim faith for such a union to take place, although any children from the marriage would need to be raised as Muslims.[97]

---

95. The response may reflect the view of Islām as a Christian heresy articulated by St. Iōannēs of Damaskos (see the citation of texts in Griffith, 42). Nevertheless, the word "communion" (κοινωνίαν, communicatio) does not signify a sharing of the Eucharist, but of a union with the Muslim partner. The same word is used regarding the requirement of sharing one religion contained in the final part of Herennius Modestinus's third-century formula to define a legal marital union, later adopted by the Byzantine church (Mommsen, 2:657): "Nuptiae sunt coniunctio maris et feminæ et consortium omnis vitæ, divini et humani juris communicatio." The formula appeared in *Code* 9.32.4 and *Digest* 23.2.1. Compare also the definition contained in the *Institutes* 1.9.1 (Krüger, 42): "Nuptiæ autem sive matrimonium est viri et mulieris coniunctio, individuam consuetudinem vitæ continens." A Greek translation of Modestinus's formula appeared in *Basilika* 28.4.1 (Scheltema, A4:1325): "Γάμος ἐστὶν ἀνδρὸς καὶ γυναικὸς συνάφεια καὶ συγκλήρωσις τοῦ βίου παντός, θείου τε καὶ ἀνθρωπίνου δικαίου κοινωνία" ("Marriage is a union of a man and woman, a consortium for all of life, a sharing of divine and human law").

As adopted by the Byzantine church, the common religion in the definition of marriage came to be identified as the faith of the Catholic Church. For general coverage of the definition and its acceptance by the Byzantine church, see Viscuso, "Nikodemos," 189–190, 204–206; compare its use by Theodōros Balsamōn and Iōannēs Zonaras (Rhallēs and Potlēs, 2:472).

96. A term used by Christian writers to refer to Muslims in general. The word is based on the name of Abraham's concubine Hagar (Gen 16), who was viewed as the biblical ancestor of the Bedouin Arab Muslim invaders of the seventh century, and later became associated with Muslims in general (Griffith, 24, n. 6).

97. The allowing of Muslim unions with *dhimmī* women is based on Qur'ān 5:5, and the prohibition with *dhimmī* men on Qur'ān 2:221. In classical Islāmic legal thought, wives were considered naturally subservient to their husbands, who are the dominant and superior members of the household. Consequently,

Another possible influence of Islāmic law can be found in a question on a former Christian who wishes to convert from Islām. Concerns regarding the Islāmic penalty of death for apostasy appear implied by the need to meet "secretly . . . with the Orthodox": "An Orthodox who, when he was taken prisoner by the Hagarenes, also under force renounced the Orthodox faith and was circumcised, almost all the time mourns over the impurity, and secretly meets with the Orthodox, and is reclaiming his salvation. Since he also wishes to partake of the Sanctified Elements, we seek to learn what to do."[98] The fact that the conversion is said to have occurred by force and while the convert was a prisoner provides further evidence of how Islāmic rule affected Christian communities.[99] The response does not

---

while there is no asymmetry involved in a Muslim husband marrying and dominating a *dhimmī* wife, the reverse case is unacceptable since a Muslim wife would not be able to enjoy her superiority as a Muslim by her wifely subservience to an infidel spouse (Friedmann, 160–193). In this way, the marriage of Muslim men with *dhimmī* women and the prohibition of the reverse is a symbol of Islāmic superiority (Friedmann, 292). Schools of classicial Islāmic legal thought generally base the requirement for children to be raised as Muslims on the premise that Islām is the natural condition into which each child is born and that non-Muslim parents transform the child afterward. Consequently, since children are Muslims in principle, in the event of intermarriage with a Muslim man or when one of their parents converts, they must raised as Muslims and, if resistant, be coerced into Islām. When separated from non-Muslim parents, such children must also be raised as Muslims (Friedmann, 109–115). Certain early Muslim jurists are of the opinion that the Muslim husband may permit the *dhimmī* wife to attend church and practice her religion. In analyzing these texts, Friedmann believes that any restrictions should be understood in a general context of eliminating "the husband's discomfort and the diminution of his enjoyment" rather than being based on a strictly religious consideration (Friedmann, 187–190).

98. Question 60. In the question, the former Orthodox does not publicly renounce the Islāmic faith by denying the oneness of God and the prophethood of Muḥammad as expressed in the declaration of Islāmic faith (the *shahāda*) whereby one becomes a Muslim, but rather seeks to practice Christianity secretly.

99. Although not the main focus of discussion regarding captives, certain classical Islāmic jurists justified the coerced conversion of non-Muslim prisoners (Friedmann, 115–120). Most legal scholars did not consider these conversions to be legitimate unless the convert retained the new faith after compulsion was removed, in which case any later reversion would be considered apostasy (ibid., 144–146). In general, early legal opinion favored execution of male apostates, some allowing the option of repentance, while females were imprisoned, whipped, or coerced into Islām (ibid., 135–139). In fact, significant legal opinion allowed for coerced conversion of females under certain conditions, unlike their male counterparts (ibid., 106–108). Most jurists held that apostates who secretly practiced the Manichean creed were to be executed,

address the problem of secrecy, but concentrates on the need for repentance and adequate preparation in order to be received:

> Crowns are for those who struggle. And our Lord and God Je-
> sus Christ said, "If anyone will confess me before men, I also
> will confess him before my Father who is in heaven."[100] In-
> deed, one who is deranged will accept an impure vessel for
> a receptacle of *myron*. For which reason the one repenting
> in this way and wishing to undergo a change for the good
> will be deemed worthy of the consolation of episcopal and
> other spiritual instruction but shall not be deemed worthy
> of the Holy Mysteries. For first he ought to be cleansed of
> the pollution of impiety and then be received; and after
> the customary time he will also become a sharer of Holy
> Communion.

The use of the word "crowns" appears to imply martyrdom, but the
response allows for flexibility in the use of episcopal instruction. Perhaps this is a diplomatic consideration in light of possible retribution
from an Islāmic regime.

That members of the Melkite community continued to be employed as administrators by the Sunnī Ayyūbid dynasty is suggested by
Question 29, "Can bishops, monks, and clergy become without danger
heads of public offices and works, and persons charged with matters of
governance, or not?" *Dhimmī* populations were sometimes tolerated
because of the special services that they provided, which could include
those professions prohibited to Muslims. This appears to be reflected
in Question 5, "Is it without danger for clergy, and indeed also laity,
to lend money at interest, or rather, is it ruinous?" and Question 27,
"Can a priest or deacon safely become a moneychanger, customs collector, physician, or astrologer, or not?" Comparative study of Arabic
texts from the period may yield further examples.

A final observation on the declining fortunes of the Melkite community may be illustrated in Question 47, concerning marriage impediments: "The land of the Alexandrians, which derives its ancestry
from and is filled with countless numbers of Orthodox Christians,
presently through divine dispensation is reduced by a moderate number of Orthodox Christians. Therefore, we seek to learn if it is per-

---

whether or not they repented or came forward without being discovered first
(ibid., 139–143). Such a consideration may have also been the case in the present question for the apostate who is attempting to practice crypto-Christianity.

    100. Matt 10:32.

missible for a marriage contract to take place within the sixth degree, on account of the necessity of the circumstances." The reduction of the community's numbers has apparently prompted consideration of marriages within prohibited degrees of kinship. Its former "countless numbers" are contrasted to the present reduction "by a moderate number," but even a "moderate" decline nevertheless proves to be an issue for those wishing to marry Melkite spouses outside the circle of their relatives.

Summary

The *Canonical Questions of the Most Holy Patriarch of Alexandria, Lord Markos, and the Answers for Them by the Most Holy Patriarch of Antioch, Lord Theodōros Balsamōn,* composed in February 1195, was an official document issued by the Holy Synod of Constantinople in reply to a series of formal inquiries made between patriarchates. Theodōros Balsamōn, a twelfth-century patriarch of Antioch in exile, did not have an ecclesial role in this exchange. Although the responses are attributed to him, Balsamōn's participation and contribution in framing answers may be seen as that of a subject matter expert in canonical and legal affairs serving the Ecumenical Patriarchate, whose Holy Synod was ultimately responsible for the decisions underlying the canonical responses.

The questions, if it can be assumed that they were composed by the Alexandrian patriarchate based on the accompanying letter of Markos III, reflect the concerns of the religious leadership of the Melkite Christian community that lived in the Arabic-speaking world of Islām in Egypt. Underlying the questions and their associated responses may have been an effort by the Melkite patriarchate to reinforce its self-identity as the Catholic Church, and thereby to affirm the legitimacy of its own authority and distinguish itself from Christian communities considered heretical.

The fact that the Alexandrian patriarchate was unable to independently resolve some issues may also reflect a declining standard of ecclesiastical discipline and clerical literacy due to its subaltern status under Islāmic rule. Such disabilities are clearly reflected in questions on restrictions governing intermarriage with Muslims and forced conversion to Islām.

The *Canonical Questions* represented an attempt by the Alexandrian patriarchate to resolve a number of canonical and liturgical problems arising in a church under Islāmic rule, and to harmonize its practices with those of the Great Church of Constantinople. In this context, the usages of Great Church were regarded as the custom of the New Rome, free from heresy as well as from the effects of Muslim or crusader domination, and thus a guide or model for another patriarchate under Islām.

OVERVIEW OF THE TRANSLATION

The following translation comprises the sixty-six canonical questions and answers attributed to Theodōros Balsamōn based on the text published by G. A. Rhallēs and M. Potlēs in the fourth volume of their Σύνταγμα τῶν θείων καὶ ἱερῶν κανόνων.[101] No critical edition of the *Canonical Questions* presently exists. Although based on an unedited text, this translation is offered to students of Byzantine canon law, history, and theology as an interim solution to the problem of the scarcity of translations. The annotations are meant to assist the reader, but are not intended to provide an exhaustive explanation. In general, the notes are used to indicate useful bibliography, identify unfamiliar names, provide dates, and explain selected passages.

In the introduction to the fourth volume of their canonical collection, Rhallēs and Potlēs stated the following regarding the text of the *Canonical Questions*:

> In this way, we first published the canonical questions of Patriarch Markos of Alexandria with Balsamōn's answers to them, which were published by Bonefidius, pt. 3, pp. 237–300,[102] and reprinted by Leunclavius, vol. 1, pp. 262–294.[103]

---

101. Rhallēs and Potlēs, 4:447–496.

102. Enimundus Bonefidius, *Iuris orientalis libri tres* ([Geneva] or [Paris]: H. Stephanus, 1573), 2:237–300.

103. Ioannes Leunclavius, *Iuris Graeco-Romani tam canonici quam civilis tomi duo* (Frankfurt: Petrus Fischer, 1596), 1:362–394. The Greek text is accompanied by the Latin translation of Bonefidius in parallel columns.

The above count the number of these questions as 64, or actually 63, on account of a numbering mistake after question 44. In the present edition, they are counted as 66, of which three, unpublished until now, were taken from the historical manuscript of Codex XXIV of the Imperial Library in Vienna, from which also many other omissions and faulty readings of editions up until now were addressed.[104]

The error in the Bonefidius and Leunclavius numbering was to skip Question 45, resulting in the count 43, 44, and 46. As stated above, the text in Rhallēs and Potlēs has corrected numbering and additional questions. The three questions added were numbered 3, 20, and 21 in the Rhallēs and Potlēs publication. The edition of Bonefidius/Leunclavius was reprinted in volume 138 of the *Patrologia Graeca*, columns 951–1012, and also in volume 119, columns 1031–1094.

In addition to the textual tradition referenced above, there exists another version of the *Canonical Questions* that differs substantially in form and content. The modern Greek scholar Manouēl Gedeōn published this version under the title *Solutions to questions of the most holy patriarch of Alexandria lord Markos which were submitted during the patriarchate of the most holy patriarch of Constantinople, lord Geōrgios Xiphilinos* (Λύσεις ἐπὶ ταῖς ἀπορίαις τοῦ ἁγιωτάτου πατριάρχου Ἀλεχανδρείας κῦρ Μάρκου ἐξενεχθεῖσαι ἐπὶ τῆς πατριαρχίας τοῦ ἁγιωτάτου πατριάρχου Κωνσταντινουπόλεως, κῦρ Γεωργίου τοῦ Ξιφιλίνου).

The variant lacks the introduction or letter of Markos III and is variously attributed in manuscripts to Balsamōn and Iōannēs of Chalcedon. Gedeōn believed the variant work to be an earlier draft by Balsamōn. Grumel, Stevens, and Katsaros refuted this viewpoint based on analyses of form and content as well as extensive examinations of the manuscript traditions associated with both versions of the questions.[105] They reached the general conclusion that the variant published by Gedeōn should be attributed to Iōannēs Kastamonitēs, a bishop of Chalcedon contemporary to Balsamōn. Speculation

104. Rhallēs and Potlēs, 4:7. The manuscript referenced is Vindob histor 24 (16th century), ff. 289ʳ–310ᵛ. For a description of the manuscript, see Herbert Hunger, *Katalog der griechischen Handschriften der Österreichischen Nationalbibiothek 1: Codices historici, codices philologici* (Vienna: Prachner; Vienna: Hollinek, 1961), 27.

105. See the publication in Gedeōn, *Nea*; and Gedeōn. See also subsequent analyses by Grumel, "Les réponses"; Stevens, 114–119; Reg, 1184; and Katsaros, 307–344.

was made that Ecumenical Patriarch Geōrgios II initially tasked Kastamonitēs, a member of the Holy Synod, with producing a version of the questions and responses, and that his resulting work was found insufficient. Consequently, Balsamōn was commissioned as a legal expert to frame a version of the questions and answers, and it was this work that was eventually accepted by the patriarch and Holy Synod.

The numbering of the questions for the editions of Rhallēs and Potlēs, and Bonefidius/Leunclavius/*Patrologia Graeca*, is presented in the following table:[106]

Rhallēs and Potlēs	Bonefidius, Leunclavius, and *Patrologia Graeca*
1	1
2	2
3	—
4	3
5	4
6	5
7	6
8	7
9	8
10	9
11	10
12	11
13	12
14	13
15	14
16	15
17	16
18	17
19	18
20	—
21	—
22	19
23	20
24	21
25	22
26	23
27	24
28	25

106. This table is based on Katsaros, 391–392.

Rhallēs and Potlēs	Bonefidius, Leunclavius, and *Patrologia Graeca*
29	26
30	27
31	28
32	29
33	30
34	31
35	32
36	33
37	34
38	35
39	36
40	37
41	38
42	39
43	40
44	41
45	42
46	43
47	44
48	46
49	47
50	48
51	49
52	50
53	51
54	52
55	53
56	54
57	55
58	56
59	57
60	58
61	59
62	60
63	61
64	62
65	63
66	64

In general, conventional English spellings will be used for place names. Names of most persons along with certain objects and concepts will be transliterated. In the text of the *Canonical Questions*, the word σχῆμα can be used to denote the outward appearance of a person and his or her status in life. Thus, in the case of monks, it can mean either the habit proper or the monastic way of life. Throughout the translation the Greek word will be retained in its transliterated form, *schēma*. The word μύρον signifies the oil of anointing employed for the sacrament or mystery of holy chrismation following holy baptism, the reception of converts as well as apostates, the consecration of holy altars, the deposit of holy relics, and other uses. This Greek word will also be retained in its transliterated form, *myron*. "Catholic Church" refers to the Orthodox communion of the four patriarchates of Constantinople, Alexandria, Antioch, and Jerusalem. "Latins" are considered those who are part of the Western church under Rome, do not share in the communion of the Catholic Church, and have alien customs and dogmas. In the *Canonical Questions* the following terms are used for the Holy Body and Blood of Christ: "Divine Sanctified Elements" (τὰ θεία ἁγιάσματα), "Sanctified Elements" (τὰ ἁγιάσματα), "Holy Elements" (τὰ ἅγια), "Good Portion" (τὸ ἀγαθόν), "Gift" (τὸ δώρημα), "Divine Mysteries" (τὰ θεία μυστήρια), "Holy Mysteries" (τὰ ἅγια μυστήρια), "Divine Sanctified Elements of Communion" (τὰ θεία ἁγιάσματα κοινωνίας), and "Divine and Holy Communion" (ἡ θεία καὶ ἁγία μετάληψις).

Select Bibliography

Modern Publications of Balsamōn's Works

Bonefidius, Enimundus. *Iuris orientalis libri tres.* [Geneva] or [Paris]: H. Stephanus, 1573.

Leunclavius, Ioannes. *Iuris Graeco-Romani tam canonici quam civilis tomi duo.* Frankfurt: Petrus Fischer, 1596.

Migne, J.-P., ed. *Patrologiae cursus completus: Series graeca.* 161 vols. in 166 pts. Paris: 1857–1866.

Ῥάλλης, Γ. Α., and Μ. Ποτλής. *Σύνταγμα θείων καὶ ἱερῶν Κανόνων τῶν τε Ἁγίων καὶ Πανευφήμων Ἀποστόλων καὶ τῶν ἱερῶν Οἰκουμενικῶν καὶ τοπικῶν Συνόδων καὶ τῶν κατὰ μέρος Ἁγίων Πατέρων.* 6 vols. Αθήνα: Γ. Χαρτοφύλαξ, 1852–1859.

Secondary Materials

Angold, Michael. *Church and Society in Byzantium under the Comneni, 1081–1261.* Cambridge: Cambridge University Press, 1995.

Darrouzès, Jean. "Le traité des transferts : Édition critique et commentaire." *Revue des études byzantines* 42 (1984): 147–214.

Gallagher, Clarence. *Church Law and Church Order in Rome and Byzantium: A Comparative Study.* Burlington, VT: Ashgate and Variorum, 2002.

Γεδεών, Μανουὴλ. "Θεοδώρου Βαλσαμῶνος λύσεων κανονικῶν διάφοροι γραφαί." Ἐκκλησιατικὴ Ἀλήθεια 35 (1915): 169–173, 177–182, 185–189.

_____. "Λύσεις ἐπὶ ταῖς ἀπορίαις τοῦ ἁγιωτάτου πατριάρχου Ἀλεχανδρείας κῦρ Μάρκου ἐξενεχθεῖσαι ἐπὶ τῆς πατριαρχίας τοῦ ἁγιωτάτου πατριάρχου Κωνσταντινουπόλεως, κῦρ Γεωργίου τοῦ Ξιφιλίνου." Νέα Βιβλιοθήκη Ἐκκλησιαστικῶν Συγγραφέων 1 (1903): 135–160.

Grumel, V. "Le Περὶ μεταθέσεων et le patriarche de Constantinople Dosithée." Études byzantines 1 (1943): 239–249.

_____. "Les réponses canoniques à Marc d'Alexandrie, leur caractère official, leur double redaction." Échos D'Orient 38 (1939): 321–333.

Hartmann, Wilfried, and Kenneth Pennington, eds. The History of Byzantine and Eastern Canon Law to 1500. Washington, DC: The Catholic University of America Press, 2012.

Herman, E. "Balsamon (Théodore)." Dictionnaire de Droit Canonique, 2:76–83.

Horna, Konstantin. "Die Epigramme des Theodoros Balsamon." Wiener Studien, Zeitschift für klassiche Philologie 25 (1903): 165–215.

Κατσάρος, Βασίλης. Ἰωάννης Κασταμονίτης, Συμβολή στη μελέτη του βίου, του ἔργου και της ἐποχῆς του. Θεσσαλονίκη: Κέντρο Βυζαντινῶν Ἐρευνῶν, 1988.

Λεονταρίτου, Βασιλική. "Μελέτη χάριν τῶν δύο ὀφφικίων, τοῦ τε χαρτοφύλακος καὶ τοῦ πρωτοφύλακος καὶ τοῦ πρωτεδίκου. Ἑρμηνευτικό πόνημα ἤ σώρευση διεκδικήσεων." In Τρωιάνος, Σπύρος, ed., Κατευόδιον: In Memoriam Nikos Oikonomides, 39–63. Αθήνα: Εκδόσεις Αντ. Ν. Σάκκουλα, 2008.

Macrides, Ruth. "Nomos and Kanon on Paper and in Court." In Morris, Rosemary, ed., Church and People in Byzantium: Society for the Promotion of Byzantine Studies; Twentieth Spring Symposium of Byzantine Studies, Manchester, 1986. Birmingham: Centre for Byzantine, Ottoman and Modern Greek Studies, University of Birmingham, 1990.

Miller, Em. "Lettres de Théodore Balsamon." Annuaire de L'Association pour L'Encouragement des Études Grecques en France 18 (1884): 8–19.

Οικονομίδης, Ν., ed. Τὸ Βυζάντιο κατὰ τὸν 12ο αιώνα: κανονικὸ δίκαιο, κράτος καὶ κοινωνία. Αθήνα: Ἐταιρεία βυζαντινῶν καὶ μεταβυζαντινῶν μελετῶν, 1991.

Petit, L. "Balsamon, Théodore." *Dictionnaire de Théologie Catholique*, 2:135–138.

Simon, Dieter. "Balsamon zum Gewohnheitsrecht." In Aerts, W. J., J. H. A. Lokin, S. L. Radt, and N. van der Wal, eds., *ΣΧΟΛΙΑ: Studia ad Criticam Interpretationemque Textum Graecorum et Historiam Iuris Graeco-Romani Pertinentia Viro Doctissimo D. Holwerda Oblata*, 119–133. Groningen, Netherlands: Egbert Forsten, 1985.

Stevens, Gerardus Petrus. *De Theodoro Balsamone, Analysis Operum ac Mentis Iuridicae*. Rome: Libreria Editrice della Pontificia Università Lateranense, 1969.

Stolte, Bernard H. "Balsamon and the Basilika." *Subseciva Groningana. Studies in Roman and Byzantine Law* 3 (1988): 115–125.

Viscuso, Patrick. *Orthodox Canon Law: A Casebook for Study*. 2nd ed. Brookline, MA: Holy Cross Orthodox Press, 2011.

_____. "Cleanliness, Not a Condition for Godliness: *Alousia* as a Canonical Requirement in Late Byzantium." *Greek Orthodox Theological Review* 46, nos. 1–2 (2001): 75–88.

_____. "Death in Late Byzantine Canon Law." *Ostkirchliche Studien* 51 (2002): 225–248.

_____. "Theodore Balsamon's Canonical Images of Women." *Greek, Roman, and Byzantine Studies* 45 (2005): 317–326.

_____. "Marital Relations in the Theology of the Byzantine Canonist Theodore Balsamon." *Ostkirchliche Studien* 39 (1990): 281–288.

PART TWO

LIST OF CANONICAL QUESTIONS

Question 1

Are the liturgies read in the areas of Alexandria and Jerusalem, and said to be composed by the holy Apostles Iakōvos the Brother of God and Markos, acceptable or not to the Holy and Catholic Church?

Question 2

Various books are found in the eastern and southern lands. Some are called "Teachings of the Holy Apostles," others "Visions of Saint Paul." Therefore, I ask whether we ought to read them.

Question 3

Are the coverings for holy chalices and holy patens, and likewise other articles of the holy table, and the vessels in which holy baptisms occur, sanctified by particular prayers, or does communion and partaking of Holy Elements suffice for their sanctification?

Question 4

The sixty books of laws, the so-called *Basilika*, were not issued in our lands, for which reason we do not know their contents. Therefore, we seek to learn whether we are consequently condemned.

Question 5

Is it without danger for clergy, and indeed also laity, to lend money at interest, or rather, is it ruinous?

Question 6

Is it without danger for Orthodox Syrians and those from Armenia, but indeed also faithful from other lands, to celebrate in their own language, or are they in every way forced to celebrate with the Greek language?

Question 7

A man betrothed a woman, and he died before being blessed with her as has been prescribed, and before uniting himself with her. Is it without danger for her to take his brother for a husband, or not?

Question 8

May a man who took another for a wife because of the death of the woman betrothed to him be deemed worthy of diaconal or priestly rank without danger of condemnation, or shall he be impeded as a digamist?

Question 9

If a priest might be tonsured, may he be permitted to exercise the priesthood after the tonsuring, or not?

Question 10

Would a layman, if he might fantasize, on the same day be considered worthy of communion of the Divine Sanctified Elements, or not? And shall a priest, if he might fantasize, exercise the priesthood on the same day as the fantasy, or not?

Question 11

May the man who unites in a fleshly manner with his legal spouse be considered worthy of partaking of the Sanctified Elements on the same day, or not?

Question 12

If a priest bathes, is he able to celebrate the liturgy on the same day? And a layman after going to the baths, may he be permitted on the same day to partake of the Mysteries? And contrariwise, shall the priest who celebrated liturgy or the layman who was deemed worthy of the Divine Sanctified Elements bathe or be bled, or not?

Question 13

If someone vomits after Holy Communion, by what tradition might he be disciplined?

Question 14

Shall one perform priestly functions or celebrate holy baptism on a ship or in an unconsecrated house without danger?

Question 15

Shall one perform priestly rites or pray together without danger with heretics, namely, Jacobites and Nestorians, in their churches or even our own, or might one share a common table with them, or perform sponsorship at holy baptism, or perform memorial services of the departed, or commune of the Divine Sanctified Elements with them? For the area's difficulties create many such things, and I seek what one must do.

Question 16

Latin prisoners and others are present in our Catholic churches and seek to partake of the Divine Sanctified Elements. We seek to learn whether this must indeed be permitted.

Question 17

Is reception of the Divine Sanctified Elements self-chosen for all clerical and lay monks who have not been impeded, so that they would be able nearly every day to be sanctified through it, or is the Gift regulated as under a rule? But also for those of them who come to church, is reception of the Good Portion required, or chosen and self-bidden?

Question 18

Are deacons who concelebrate with an archpriest or priest necessarily obliged to partake of Communion, or not?

Question 19

Is it without danger for the administration and reception of the Divine Sanctified Elements to take place with cold wine and water? Or is it necessary also for hot water to be placed into the Holy Things at the time of reception?

Question 20

If one might let fall anything on the ground from the holy chalice or holy paten, what censure shall the one performing priestly functions in this case be placed under?

Question 21

Is it allowed for an unordained monk, or even one who is ordained, to receive a confession from men on his own?

Question 22

Does a secular priest rightly undertake confessions of any men
with episcopal permission, or not?

Question 23

Is it without danger of condemnation that monks change to other
monasteries from the monasteries where they were tonsured, or not?

Question 24

Is it allowed for anyone to be a clergyman in different churches,
or not?

Question 25

An ancient custom prevailed in the land of Alexandria that deceased priests and hierarchs are anointed with holy *myron* and buried. We seek to learn whether this is without danger of condemnation.

Question 26

May the mutilated or one-eyed be deemed worthy of priestly
rank, or shall the one who suffered illness after ordination also exercise the priesthood after the affliction, or not?

Question 27

Can a priest or deacon safely become a moneychanger, customs
collector, physician, or astrologer, or not?

Question 28

A Monothelite who has a priestly religious profession turned by
repentance toward the Orthodox faith among us, and was received,
and was sanctified. After a short time, returning to his own vomit,
he became a heretic as before. And again, as he states, after being by
himself, and perceiving the sin, he returned to the Orthodox faith,
and was received, in the manner of the prodigal who rightly returned.
Since he also wishes even to be deemed worthy of the priesthood, we
seek to learn what is to be done.

Question 29

Can bishops, monks, and clergy become without danger heads of public offices and works, and persons charged with matters of governance, or not?

Question 30

A married couple chose the monastic life by perhaps a common desire and allurement for profit of the soul. Since they are living in one dwelling again, living together in every way and sharing the same table, I seek to learn what to do against them.

Question 31

If hierarchs who, when they ordain deacons and priests, but indeed also when they sanctify children of Orthodox through divine baptism or even certain heretics, and likewise distribute the Divine Sanctified Elements to them, might require from them on account of their efforts a certain amount of money, are they acting correctly, or not?

Question 32

Should those who come through recognition of the truth to the Orthodox faith, namely, Nestorians, Armenians, Jacobites, and other heretics, be made perfect by holy *myron* alone or also by divine baptism?

Question 33

If a heretical priest or deacon might be deemed worthy of divine and holy baptism, or of sanctification by holy *myron*, shall he serve as a priest with his prior ordination, or might he be deemed worthy of another ordination if he wishes to serve as a priest?

Question 34

If the wife and children of a man who came to the faith of the Orthodox from heresy, or even others related and sharing the same household with him, will not become Orthodox, but cling to the former heresy, shall the man perfected, as has been stated, through baptism, not be prohibited from ascending to priestly or episcopal rank? Or shall he also be deprived of such good on account of their evil?

Question 35

Is it without danger of condemnation for sponsorships of children to be performed by Latins, Armenians, Monothelites, Nestorians, and other such ones, or rather something hateful and to be averted?

Question 36

Orthodox women are apparently joined in marriage with Saracens or even with heretics and wish, like Orthodox as they assert, to partake of the Divine Sanctified Elements. Therefore, we seek to learn what to do.

Question 37

Some women who preside over female monasteries seek episcopal permission on account of hearing the confessions of the nuns under them. Therefore, we seek whether it is possible for this to take place.

Question 38

The divine canons have made mention of deaconesses. Therefore, we seek to learn what is their ministry.

Question 39

Are deacons and subdeacons able to be legally united with wives, or not?

Question 40

Is it permissible for priests who are abbots, or chief priests (πρωτοπαπάδας) and hierarchs, to be honored by *epimanika* and *epigonatia*, or has it been prohibited?

Question 41

By reason of an ancient indigenous custom, corpses of Orthodox are buried in our local churches. Therefore, I seek to learn whether this is without danger of condemnation.

Question 42

Inhabitants (κατοικοί) of certain parishes (ἐνοριῶν) who requested ordination from their own hierarchs are approaching bishops of other parishes, and are ordained, as each one desires. I seek to learn if indeed this takes places safely for them.

Question 43

Are deacons able to be deemed worthy of priestly rank contrary to the opinion of their archdeacon, or not?

Question 44

Shall laymen who married a second time be considered legally fit for another marriage, that is, a third one, or not?

Question 45

Is partaking of the Divine Sanctified Elements permitted for concubines, or not?

Question 46

Until what degree is the affinity (συμπενθερία) of co-parents an impediment?

Question 47

The land of the Alexandrians, which derives its ancestry from and is filled with countless numbers of Orthodox Christians, presently through divine dispensation is reduced by a moderate number of Orthodox Christians. Therefore, we seek to learn if it is permissible for a marriage contract to take place within the sixth degree, on account of the necessity of the circumstances.

Question 48

If a man might fornicate with a Christian woman prisoner, also Orthodox like him, shall he sell her as a slave without danger?

Question 49

If an Orthodox might commit fornication with a Jewish or Hagarene woman, might he be corrected through penance, or shall he be rebaptized?

Question 50

At what age might a man or woman be accepted for confession?

Question 51

If spouses might have fleshly relations during the night of the first day that bears the name of the Lord, shall they be penanced as those who act unlawfully, or not?

Question 52
If during the forty-day fast spouses did not live in chastity, shall they be worthy of the Divine Sanctified Elements of Communion on the world-saving feast of Pascha, or not?

Question 53
Is it without danger on the day that bears the name of the Lord to go to the baths and to cleanse oneself with warm water, or not?

Question 54
Is the man who breaks his fast with meat, cheese, and eggs on Wednesdays and Fridays throughout the whole year pardonable, or not?

Question 55
Are the fasts of the feasts of the Holy Apostles, the Nativity of Christ, the Dormition of the Holy Theotokos, and the Savior required, or optional and unimportant?

Question 56
Shall those who abstain during these fasts, and in addition also those who eat dry foods on Wednesdays and Fridays, be given a second meal to care for bodily need, or not?

Question 57
On the eve before the feast of the Raising from the Dead of the Righteous Lazaros, and on a feast of saints during Lent, shall one celebrate a Divine Liturgy without danger, or not? Likewise also during the entire holy forty-day fast, is it possible to baptize, or to perform benedictions of marriages and betrothals, or not?

Question 58
Do ordinations of subdeacons, deacons, priests, and hierarchs take place during holy and Great Lent without danger, or not?

Question 59
Shall things of any kind or even fruits offered by anyone in the holy churches of God be received and held under authority by someone? And what and which are the ecclesiastical taxes (κανονικά) given annually to priests and hierarchs?

Question 60

An Orthodox who, when he was taken prisoner by the Hagarenes, also under force renounced the Orthodox faith and was circumcised, almost all the time mourns over the impurity, and secretly meets with the Orthodox, and is reclaiming his salvation. Since he also wishes to partake of the Sanctified Elements, we seek to learn what to do.

Question 61

A mob of peasants present me with one who appears to them to be worthy of episcopal or priestly rank and implacably demand that he be confirmed and ordained a hierarch or deacon. Therefore, I seek to learn whether we are compelled to comply with the cries of the crowds.

Question 62

Shall children born from a second marriage, slave women, and concubines be deemed worthy of the priesthood, or not?

Question 63

A reader who was entrusted by an abbot to manage monastery properties wishes to preside over priests who are there and other clergy, and to be commemorated with the abbot in the sacred services. Accordingly, I ask to learn whether he is asserting himself in a good way concerning this.

Question 64

If a rural priest might perform a benediction of a third marriage, while knowing that it was a third marriage, may he be punished, or as a peasant shall he be deemed worthy of pardon?

Question 65

A woman who was being forced by her own father to be legally joined with a husband, and upon seeing the union being guaranteed by her father through written contracts, sent information of the marriage taking place to a man who was erotically attracted to her. The good-for-nothing man, as one maddened by love, arrived one evening at the house of the woman with some of his low-class companions and abducted her willingly, and brought her back to his house, which is situated in the area of another village. Therefore, I ask to learn whether those who so organized such abduction can be joined canonically through a benediction. For the parents of the woman also wish presently for this to take place.

Question 66

A wife who fell seriously ill threw herself into the sea during an evening hour and drank the cup of death apparently in order to relieve herself from the suffering of the disease. Therefore, her husband, who is a reader, both then and at present asked whether he is henceforth impeded from priestly rank.

CANONICAL QUESTIONS
Of the Most Holy Patriarch of Alexandria,
Lord Markos,
And the Answers for Them
By the Most Holy Patriarch of Antioch,
LORD THEODŌROS BALSAMŌN

The seer of God and prophet Moses said, "Ask your father and he will tell you, your elders and they will speak to you."[1] Lord Markos, the most holy patriarch of Alexandria,[2] Our Mediocrity's beloved brother and concelebrant, who is father of fathers, by the grace of God, and elder of elders, thereupon not having this prophetic saying chanted for him, because there was internal strife over many ecclesiastical questions, accepted another oracle from the same *kinnor* (κινύρα)[3] of the Spirit, which states, "Behold what is so good or what so delightful, than for brothers to be of the same mind?"[4] For which reason, just as an instrument requiring a musician's care, setting forth a query in writing, he entrusted this to Our Mediocrity. He sought that the canonical questions and problems contained in it be discussed in common and that this book of fraternal response be written. Indeed, the letter composed by His Holiness expressly states the following:

> In the name of the Father, and the Son, and the Holy Spirit. Questions that the Christians dwelling in the land of the Saracens[5] and their possessions ask, which were posed by

---

1. Deut 32:7 (LXX).
2. Markos III, patriarch of Alexandria (1180–1209).
3. Κινύρα, derived from Hebrew and found in the Septuagint, is a stringed instrument or lyre.
4. Ps 132:1 (LXX).
5. A term used by Christian writers to refer to Muslims in general. Its origins are disputed by modern scholarship (Griffith, 24, n. 6). The modern

Markos of Alexandria, the most humble among patriarchs, in the days of our most pious and beloved of Christ emperor Lord Isaakios Angelos,[6] and during the reign of the most holy and ecumenical patriarch Lord Geōrgios,[7] whose years may God increase in length of days. In the month of February of the thirteenth indiction, 1,203[8] years after the incarnation of our Lord and God and Savior Jesus Christ.

Question 1

Are the liturgies read in the areas of Alexandria and Jerusalem, and said to be composed by the holy Apostles Iakōvos the Brother of God and Markos, acceptable or not to the Holy and Catholic Church?

Response

The great apostle Paul, the rhetorician and teacher of God's holy churches, instructing the Corinthians, states, "I appeal to you brethren, by the name of our Lord Jesus Christ, that all of you agree that there be no dissensions among you, but that you be united in the same mind and the same judgment."[9] Therefore, we say that neither by Holy Scripture nor a canon set forth in a council were we taught that the holy Apostle Markos handed down a sacred rite. Only canon 32 of the holy and ecumenical council held in the Trullo[10] of

---

scholar Raymond Le Coz suggested various sources for its etymological derivation (Le Coz, 92–93).

    6. Isaakios II Angelos, emperor (1185–1195, 1203–1204).

    7. Geōrgios II Xiphilinos, patriarch of Constantinople (1191–1198).

    8. = 1195.

    9. 1 Cor 1:10.

    10. In the *Canonical Questions* the Council in Trullo is considered an extension of the Sixth Ecumenical Council. It was held in 691/692, and called "in Trullo" since its assembly was held under the dome (τροῦλλος) of the great imperial palace in Constantinople. In the *Canonical Questions* the council is not associated with the Fifth Ecumenical Council or called by the name Πενθέκτη ("Fifth-sixth") even though the fathers of Trullo in their address (Προσφωνητικὸς λόγος) to Ioustinianos II Rhinotmētos, emperor (685–695, 705–711), considered themselves as completing the work of the previous two ecumenical councils by promulgating canons (Rhallēs and Potlēs, 2:298). See the analysis of Heinz Ohme in Hartmann, 77–84, and for an Orthodox perspective on the ecumenicity of Trullo, see Durǎ. According to Nicolae Durǎ, Balsamōn was the first to use the term Πενθέκτη (Fifth-sixth) as a title for this council in his commentaries based on the understanding that Trullo supplemented what was lacking in the two previous ecumenical councils (Rhallēs and Potlēs, 2:300). A text of its canons based on the edition of Joannou is reproduced with an English translation in Nedungatt, 43–186.

the Great Palace states that Iakōvos the Brother of God composed a mystical celebration. Canon 85 of the holy and all-praiseworthy apostles, and canon 59 of the Council in Laodicea,[11] which enumerated the books of the Old and New Testaments, even indeed the very apostolic writings themselves, that ought to be followed by us, do not at all make mention of the Liturgy of St. Iakōvos or St. Markos.[12] But

---

11. The local council in Laodicea is generally dated between 343 and 381.

12. Apostolic canon 85 lists the following books:

> Moses—5 books: Genesis, Exodus, Leviticus, Numbers, Deuteronomy
> Jesus of Nun
> Judges—3 books
> Ruth
> Kings—4 books
> Chronicles—2 books
> Esdra—2 books
> Esther
> Maccabees—3 books
> Job
> Psalms
> Solomon—3 books: Proverbs, Ecclesiastes, Song of Songs
> Prophets—12 books
> Isaiah
> Jeremiah
> Ezekiel
> Daniel
> Wisdom of Sirach (recommended for instruction of the young)
> Four Gospels: Matthew, Mark, Luke, John
> Paul—14 epistles
> Peter—2 epistles
> John—3 epistles
> James—1 epistle
> Jude—1 epistle
> Clement—2 epistles
> Constitutions of Clement in eight books
> Acts of the Apostles

> Laodicea, canon 59, does not list individual books. The list presented by Laodicea, canon 60, is the following:
> > Genesis, Exodus, Leviticus, Numbers, Deuteronomy
> > Jesus of Nun
> > Judges
> > Ruth
> > Esther
> > Kings—4 books
> > Chronicles—2 books

also the Catholic Church of the most holy and ecumenical throne of Constantinople does not at all recognize these. Therefore, we declare (ψηφιζόμεθα) that they are not acceptable. For even if they were, we would declare them completely in disuse, as also many other things, and this is clear from canon 85 of the holy and all-praiseworthy apostles and canon 2 of the holy and ecumenical council held in the Trullo of the Great Palace. For the former, that is to say, the apostolic, legislates that the two epistles of Clement and his Constitutions in eight books are recognized, but are not to be published, on account of the secret matters in them, while the latter does not desire them to be recognized on account of the many falsehoods and things foreign to piety inserted into them by heretics. On account of this, all the churches of God ought to follow the custom of New Rome, that is, Constantinople, and to celebrate according to the traditions of the great teachers and luminaries of piety St. Iōannēs Chrysostomos and St. Basileios. For chapter 41 of title 1 of book 2 of the *Basilika* states, "Concerning cases where there is no written law, one ought to observe the custom that Rome has used."[13]

> Esdra—2 books
> Psalms
> Proverbs
> Ecclesiastes
> Song of Songs
> Job
> Prophets—12 books
> Isaiah
> Jeremiah
> Baruch
> Lamentations
> Ezekiel
> Daniel
> Four Gospels: Matthew, Mark, Luke, John
> Acts of the Apostles
> Seven Catholic Epistles (James—1 epistle, Peter—2 epistles, John—3 epistles, Jude—1 epistle)
> Paul—14 epistles

13. A synopsis of *Basilika* 2.1.41 (Scheltema, A1:19), which reads, "Concerning cases where a written law does not apply, one must observe custom and usage. And if this is deficient, one must follow what is proximate and similar to what is required. If also neither these things are found, then one must observe the custom that Rome has used. Old usage is observed in place of law. Just as the setting forth of law either is written or unwritten, so also its abolition either takes place through written law, or through the unwritten, that is to say, through disuse." The synopsis appears to significantly change the meaning of

the passage in question by omitting any place for the following of local ancient custom and usage, in this case, that of Alexandria, in favor of following solely the custom of Rome, which is equated to that of Constantinople the New Rome in the response above, when there is a lack of applicable written law. Cf. Ioustinianos, *Digest* 1.3.32.

Regarding the visit of the patriarch of Alexandria to Constantinople and his attempted use of the Liturgy either of St. Iakōvos or St. Markos, see Balsamōn's commentary on Trullo 32 (Rhallēs and Potlēs, 2:375–378):

> The Armenians, along with other heresies similar to them, have used only wine in the Holy Mysteries, and say that they do this following the writings of the great teacher of the Church, Iōannēs the Golden-Tongued, in his explanation of the Gospel according to Matthew, which state that water is not added to the holy chalice, but wine, notwithstanding that the saint does not teach that the addition takes place by wine alone. Indeed the holy fathers, when forbidding that the sacrifice take place in this way among the Armenians, determined that wine and water be added to the sacred chalice, interpreting the words of Chysostomos not to be understood in the sense of what is being said by the Armenians, but to be written in refutation of the heresy of the *Hydroparastatai*, who add only water to the holy chalice. Gathering together what was decided concerning them, from many others, indeed even from the liturgy that was handed down from our aforementioned holy father, and from Basileios the Great, they subjected to defrocking bishops and priests who do not make the sacrifice of the holy chalice through a union of water and wine. They prescribed these things when inspired by God, for during the divine passion of our God and Savior Jesus Christ, his divine side when pierced by the spear produced not only blood but also water in order to signify the union of his two natures as unconfused. Therefore note that two heresies are refuted by the present canon. The first is the *Hydroparastatai*, who use water alone in the sacrifice of the holy chalice. The other is that of the Armenians, who do this by wine alone. Since not only the Armenians but also the Latins attack the addition of *zeon* into the holy chalice, saying that this was not received by scriptural or canonical injunction and therefore takes place in an evil way, and in a manner contrary to this divine tradition, which prescribed that by water and wine the addition of the holy chalice takes place. Let them hear that the *zeon* that is added does not change the union of the holy chalice by water and wine, neither is it anything other than water. It is added in assurance that what flowed from the holy side of our Lord Jesus Christ is life-giving, namely the blood and water, and not dead, because the greatness of the miracle is represented by this. For while from a dead body warm blood does not naturally flow, warm blood and water flowed forth from the body of the Lord, even after death, as life-giving from a life-giving body. However, if one might say, and for what reason is the *zeon* not put into the union

before consecrating the holy chalice, but after the consecration? Listen, because if the *zeon* were put in during the time of the union, it would begin to cool up to the time of Holy Communion, and the thing would end up as before. Indeed for this cause, the *zeon* is put into the holy chalice after the elevation, and the faithful partake of it as life-giving. Some Georgian priests do not put *zeon* into the holy chalice, [priests] who are most Orthodox no matter what. And when being asked one time in a synod how they do this, they said, never has any Georgian used warm water in a drink of wine by the long-held custom of the country, and on account of this neither do they use *zeon* in the Holy Elements. After being instructed in the power of the Mystery, they were commanded to place mandatorily *zeon* in the holy chalice during the time of Holy Communion. Note from the present canon that first of all St. Iakōvos the Brother of God, as the one who was the first hierarch of the Church of Jerusalem, handed down the divine sacred rite, which is unknown among us and is used among the Jerusalemites and Palestinians during great feasts. The Alexandrians say there is even a divine sacred rite of St. Markos, which also they use very much. During a synod, and much more also before the holy emperor, I discussed this when the patriarch of Alexandria stayed in the capital. For when he was about to celebrate liturgy with us and the Ecumenical Patriarch (οἰκουμενικοῦ) in the Great Church, he began to hold in his hand the liturgical book (κοντάκιον) of the Liturgy of Iakōvos, but was prohibited by him (αὐτοῦ) [trans. note: the Ecumenical Patriarch], and consented to celebrate liturgy (ὑπέσχετο λειτουργεῖν) just as also us.

Rhallēs and Potlēs also provides the following variant text for the end of the commentary in stating, "This note is thus in the manuscript codex of Trebizond" (Rhallēs and Potlēs, 2:377–378):

Note that from the present canon 32 it appears that the divine sacred service was also handed down from St. Iakōvos the Brother of God, who was the first hierarch of the Church of Jerusalem, which presently neither is found nor known among us, as it is disused. How the clergy in Palestine celebrate liturgy with the mystagogy (μυσταγωγίας) that was handed down, as they say, from the same Brother of God, and the bishops in Alexandria and the priests perform sacred services with prayers, as they say, that were handed down by St. Markos, and do not follow what is being done by the clergy throughout the empire (οἰκουμένη), that is to say, they do not pay attention to the mystagogies (μυσταγωγιῶν) handed down from St. Basileios and St. Iōannēs Chrysostomos, I do not know. This was discussed by me both in the synod and much more also at the imperial court (βασιλικοῦ βήματος) when the patriarch of Alexandria was staying in the capital, and when he was about to concelebrate with us, he wished to celebrate with the sacred rite handed down, as he said, from St. Markos, even if he was corrected not by deposition,

Question 2

Various books are found in the eastern and southern lands. Some are called, "Teachings of the Holy Apostles," others, "Visions of Saint Paul." Therefore, I ask whether we ought to read them.

Response

Since our Lord and God and Savior Jesus Christ said in the Gospels, "Take heed that you are not led astray. For many will come in my name, saying, 'I am he, and the time draws near,'"[14] we also declare (ψηφιζόμεθα καὶ ἡμεῖς) that the Church of God recognizes and confesses as apostolic teachings, visions, and constitutions the books that are set forth in apostolic canon 85 and that are believed to be the words of God's heralds, and [the Church] does not know any other apostolic writing than these.[15] Therefore, take care to avoid the innovations of the heretics, which lead astray, for they are bitterer than wormwood, even if they profess to be a bee house by a title with the names of the holy apostles.

Question 3

Are the coverings for holy chalices and holy patens, and likewise other articles of the holy table, and the vessels in which holy baptisms occur, sanctified by particular prayers, or does communion and partaking of the Holy Elements suffice for their sanctification?

Response

It is written, "Abraham believed in God and it was reckoned for him as righteousness."[16] For which reason, we also believe (διὸ καὶ ἡμεῖς πιστεύομεν) chalice coverings, paten coverings, and so forth are sanctified at the time when they are placed on the holy altar, and cover the Holy Elements, and do not require particular prayers for

---

for which everything seemed sufficient [in this way], but only by the patriarch telling him to no longer do this.

Patriarch Markos III's attempted use of a liturgy (whether that of St. Iakōvos or St. Markos) different from that being used by other celebrants took place in the cathedral church of the Ecumenical Patriarchate. The patriarch of Constantinople would be fully within his prerogatives to enforce consistency of usage during a celebration in the Church of St. Sophia, especially in the basic question of which liturgical text should be used.

14. Luke 21:8.

15. Although ascribed to the apostles and included in Byzantine collections of canons, the "apostolic canons" originated during the last quarter of the fourth century in Syria; see Menevisoglou, *Historical*, 101–124.

16. Gen 15:6 (LXX).

sanctification. In addition, one should know that all sacred things (ἱερὰ) are holy (ἄγια), but not all holy things (ἄγια) are also sacred (ἱερὰ). For the sign of the cross on coins is holy, but is not sacred. On this account, the one stealing coins that bear a venerable cross, or even the very adulated portrait of our Lord Jesus Christ, is condemned as a thief, but is not guilty of sacrilege. For chapter 1 of title 3 of book 46 of the *Basilika* clearly states, "Sacred things belong to divine law and are not subject to ownership. A sacred thing is dedicated publicly, for things individually possessed are not sacred."[17] At any rate, whatever is presented by anyone to the Catholic churches, or to the divine temples of monasteries, namely, coverings for holy chalices and holy patens, but also any other vessels, even icons within the hands of a bishop or priest, at this point when dedicated to God they become holy and sacred (ἄγια καὶ ἱερά). Whatever such things some have in their unconsecrated oratory houses are holy (ἄγια) as when they partake of the Divine Sanctified Elements and are not regarded as common. They are not sacred things (ἱερὰ) because they belong to individual persons.

Question 4

The sixty books of laws, the so-called *Basilika*, were not issued in our lands, for which reason we do not know their contents. Therefore, we seek to learn whether we are consequently condemned.

Response

According to the great apostle, "Whatever the law says, it says to those under the law."[18] Indeed, those boasting of an Orthodox life, whether they might be from the East, or from Alexandria, or elsewhere, are called Romans, and must be governed according to laws, but are not bound by the law that states, "A Roman man must not be ignorant of law."[19] For only the inhabitants of Rome, namely, the Queen of Cities, which is fortified with suitable towers and rich with many legal scholars, are bound by their fetters. For which reason, those who claim to be ignorant of the law are not pardoned, whether they might be craftsmen, or vagabonds, and ignorant of letters, since

---

17. This is a summary of *Basilika* 46.3.1 (Scheltema, A6:2124) and *Basilika* 46.3.5 (Scheltema, A6:2125); cf. *Digest* 1.8.1, 6.

18. Rom 3:19.

19. This appears to be a maxim based on *Basilika* 2.4.21 (Scheltema, A1:71); cf. *Code* 1.18.12. The phrase "from the East" may be a reference to Balsamōn's own patriarchate of Antioch.

they are able to learn the content of the law from their fellow in-habitants.[20] Those who live outside of Rome, namely, peasants and the rest, much more Alexandrians, who do not know the civil law, are pardoned. At any rate, it is good for them to ask and learn legal prescriptions. However, if it is hard to manage, they shall be worthy of pardon.

Question 5

Is it without danger for clergy, and indeed also laity, to lend money at interest, or rather, is it ruinous?

Response

The Mosaic Law states, "You shall not lend your silver to your brother."[21] The civil law approves interest at *hekatostē*, *hēmiekatostē*, and *tritē hekatostē*. For it determines that those of senatorial rank receive interest at *tritē hekatostē*, that is to say, four *nomismata* for each pound; commoners, merchants, and the rest, at *hēmiekatostē*, that is to say, six *nomismata* for each pound; those who make a mari-time loan, at twelve *nomismata* for each pound. It is not the time to explain why the interest is called *hekatostē*, when a pound does not equal one hundred *nomismata*, but seventy-two, lest this secondary subject become the main topic.[22] The latter points concern the la-ity. It is absolutely forbidden for clergy to charge interest. For canon 44 of the holy apostles clearly states this: "Let a bishop, presbyter, or deacon who lends requiring interest cease, or be defrocked." And canon 17 of the Holy First Ecumenical Council states the following in detail: "Since many enrolled in the clergy, who pursue greed and dishonest gain, forgot the divine word, which states, 'Do not lend your silver at interest,'[23] and when lending they require a percentage,

---

20. According to Paul Magdalino, the response reflects the ideological no-tion of the empire of Rome as an association of cities within which Constanti-nople was considered the queen or reigning city and extension of the state and its law. Magdalino sees in the response evidence of the alienation of Constanti-nople from the provinces or countryside (see Magdalino, "Constantinople").

21. Deut 23:19 (LXX), a paraphrase.

22. A *nomisma* was a standard gold coin; calculations are for pounds of gold. *Hekatostē* may be translated "hundredth" in order to understand Balsamōn's comment "It is not the time to explain why the interest is called *hekatostē*, when a pound does not equal one hundred *nomismata*, but seventy-two." For additional information on canonical views regarding interest rates, see Laiou.

23. Ps 14:5 (LXX).

the holy and great council decided that if anyone might be found after this decision taking interest from loans, whether otherwise exploiting the matter, or requiring half, or contriving anything else on account of dishonest gain, he shall be defrocked from the clergy and will be removed from rank." Canon 4 of the Council in Laodicea and others also state the same things.

Question 6

Is it without danger for Orthodox Syrians and those from Armenia,[24] but indeed also faithful from other lands, to celebrate in their own language, or are they in every way forced to celebrate with the Greek language?

Response

The great apostle Paul, writing to the Romans, states, "Or is God the God of Jews only and not also of Gentiles? Yes, of Gentiles also."[25] At any rate, those who are Orthodox in all things, even if they might be wholly bereft of Greek speech, shall celebrate in their own language with precise copies of the customary holy prayers translated from liturgical books (κοντακίων) with well-copied Greek letters.

Question 7

A man betrothed a woman, and he died before being blessed with her as has been prescribed, and before uniting himself with her. Is it without danger for her to take his brother for a husband, or not?

Response

The good is not good unless it occurs in a good manner. Indeed if the engagement, namely, the betrothal, was completed in accordance with the rule of the new legislation of the celebrated emperor Lord Alexios Komnēnos,[26] with a celebration of the customary holy prayers, the woman being twelve years of age, and the man completing his thirteenth year, his brother shall not take her in marriage. For

---

24. This reflects the existence of Armenian and Syriac speakers who accepted the Christological teachings of the Fourth Ecumenical Council of Chalcedon (451), unlike the majority of their respective communities. Griffith mentions the activity of Chalcedonian Armenians in Jerusalem from the seventh century onward and the Syriac Maronite community that entered into communion with the Church of Rome in 1182 (Griffith, 137, 140).

25. Rom 3:29.

26. Alexios I Komnēnos, emperor (1081–1118), Novel 24 (Zepos, 1:305–309; Dölger, 1116).

the *arrabōn*,[27] which is so finalized in every case for legal marriage, is identical. However, if according to the prevailing custom, as we learn (ὡς μανθάνομεν), in nearly all the areas south and east, the one who died pledged the property in another manner, his brother may be united legally with her.

Question 8

May a man who took another for a wife because of the death of the woman betrothed to him be deemed worthy of diaconal or priestly rank without danger of condemnation, or shall he be impeded as a digamist?

Response

If the man who was joined to another woman after her death betrothed the deceased fiancée in accordance with the rule of the cited novel,[28] he may not be deemed worthy of any rank of those of the *bēma*, for he is reckoned a digamist.[29] If he betrothed the deceased woman contrary to its provisions, he shall be ordained free from impediment, since he is not reckoned a digamist.

Question 9

If a priest might be tonsured, may he be permitted to exercise the priesthood after the tonsuring, or not?

Response

Canon 2 of the Holy and Ecumenical Council held in the most holy cathedral of Constantinople[30] states the following word for word: "Even if up to now some hierarchs who descended into a monastic *schēma* were forced to remain at the height of the hierarchy, they were overlooked while doing this. Therefore, this Holy and Ecumenical Council, correcting this oversight and remedying this disorderly practice in accordance with ecclesiastical laws, decreed that if any bishop, or any other of hierarchal rank, would wish to descend to the monastic life, and to occupy a place of penitence, he shall no longer

---

27. *Arrha sponsalicia*, "engagement gift."

28. Alexios I Komnēnos, *Novel* 24 (Zepos, 1:305–309; Dölger, 1116).

29. Since the *bēma* is the sanctuary or area of the church containing the altar, "those of the *bēma*" refers to clergy who serve the altar.

30. Holy Wisdom (879–880), canon 2. Holy Wisdom is recognized here as the Ninth Ecumenical Council. The circumstances of the council are summarized in Hartmann, 149–150. The council recognized Phōtios the Great as patriarch of Constantinople during his second reign (877–886).

then lay claim to hierarchical dignity. For the vows of monks promise obedience and discipleship, but not teaching and presidency, nor do they promise to shepherd others, but to be shepherded. Wherefore, consistent with the preceding, we decree that no longer may any of those pastors also enrolled in the hierarchical list lower himself to the place of the pastored and penitent. If anyone might dare to do this after the promulgation and decree of the decision that has presently been announced, he shall no longer return to his former office, which he set aside by his actions, depriving himself of hierarchal rank." It is understood that before the promulgation of this canon not only those of the *bēma*,[31] namely, subdeacons, deacons, and priests, but also hierarchs themselves, exercised the priesthood even after tonsure. Indeed, while hierarchs, who are separated with canonical strictness from the priesthood on account of entering the place of discipleship and repentance after tonsure, are henceforth also removed from the teaching office, priests (and simply, those of the *bēma*) shall exercise in every way the rights of rank without encumbrance even after tonsure. For both before the tonsuring and likewise also after the tonsuring, they were and are disciples and under obedience.

Question 10

Would a layman, if he might fantasize, on the same day be considered worthy of communion of the Divine Sanctified Elements,[32] or not? And shall a priest, if he might fantasize, exercise the priesthood on the same day as the fantasy, or not?

Response

The Sacred Word states, "The archpriest who offers gifts and sacrifices is chosen from among men, and just as he offers to God on the people's behalf, so indeed also on his own behalf, since the weight of fleshly weakness is laid upon him."[33] But the Lord also said through Moses, "Let the pure ones come to the pure, but the one who has a stain on his soul shall not approach my veil, and does not draw near to my altar."[34] Wherefore also three most holy patriarchs of the Alexandrian see, namely, St. Dionysios (who replies to Bishop

---

31. Since the *bēma* is the sanctuary or area of the church containing the altar, "those of the *bēma*" refers to clergy who serve the altar.

32. Holy Body and Blood of Christ.

33. A paraphrase of Heb 5:1–3.

34. A paraphrase of Lev 21:23 (LXX).

Basileiadēs), Athanasios the Great (who prescribes certain things for a monk named Amoun), and St. Timotheos (who replies to those questioning him concerning such subjects), resolved matters before concerning laity consistent with the divine Scriptures.[35] For the response of St. Dionysios states,[36] "If he is subject to desire of a woman, he should not. However, if Satan tempts him in order by this pretense he might be deprived of communion of the Mysteries, he should be communed, since the adversary tempting him will not cease attacking him during that time." For which reason, while we (ἡμεῖς) also determine (διοριζόμενοι) the same things concerning the laity, we decide (διαγινώσκομεν) not to follow the same pattern concerning bishops, deacons, and priests who fantasize through a satanic assault alone. Rather, we declare (ψηφιζόμεθα) that the celebration of the liturgy (τὴν τῆς ἱεροτελεστίας ἐνέργειαν) is prohibited for them on only the day of the dream, out of respect for the priesthood; unless the delay is perhaps dangerous, or because of the day's conspicuousness, or because of the thing's beneficialness, for then the attacker's snare is shattered, and the celebration's (ἱερουγία) power is exalted.

Question 11
May the man who unites in a fleshly manner with his legal spouse be considered worthy of partaking of the Sanctified Elements[37] on the same day, or not?

Response
Paul the herald of God, the teacher of the Church, states, "Let each one prepare himself and so let him eat from the bread and drink from the cup."[38] And again, "Let spouses not deprive one another, unless by agreement, when they are about to approach for prayer of Holy Communion."[39] And when David and his companions sought to eat from the loaves of preparation, the archpriest ascertained whether they were pure from the bed of a woman.[40] And in the Mosaic book of Exodus, the following is specifically stipulated: "And the Lord said

---

35. St. Dionysios the Great, pope of Alexandria (d. 264/265); St. Athanasios I, the Great, pope of Alexandria (b. 295, pope 328–373); and St. Timotheos I, pope of Alexandria (d. 385).

36. Incorrect reference: this should be Timotheos of Alexandria, Question 12 (Rhallēs and Potlēs, 4:338).

37. Holy Body and Blood of Christ.

38. 1 Cor 11:28.

39. 1 Cor 7:5 (an interpretation rather than a citation).

40. 1 Kgdms 21:5 (LXX) (a reference, not an exact citation).

to Moses, 'Go down to command this people, and cleanse them today and tomorrow, and let them wash their clothes and make themselves ready for the third day. For on the third day, the Lord will descend upon the Mountain of Sinai, before all the people.'"[41] And again, "Moses descended from the mountain to the people, and cleansed them. And they washed their clothes. And he said to the people, 'Make yourselves ready: for three days do not approach a woman.'"[42] The most holy patriarch of Alexandria Timotheos, when asked concerning this, stated, "Spouses who have fleshly relations ought not to be considered worthy of partaking the Divine Sanctified Elements on the very day of their fleshly intercourse."[43] For which reason, in agreement with what was so determined, we say that communion of the Sanctified Elements is not permitted for spouses on the day that they united in a fleshly manner. We also add that since the same Timotheos the Great, when asked on what day of the week ought spouses to be abstinent, answered, on Saturday and Sunday,[44] because the spiritual sacrifice is offered to the Lord on those days, by necessity the spouses ought to refrain from fleshly communion with one another on the day of partaking of the Divine Sanctified Elements, and not only the day before its observance, but also the day after it. We also pray that what takes place in an evil manner contrary to divine ordinances and teachings among those escorting the bride during the bridal procession is corrected. For after they are blessed and deemed worthy of the Divine Sanctified Elements, those delighting in the pleasures of marriage hasten to fleshly union, not considering the might of the celebration, and the disdain of the Sanctified Elements. Therefore, without exception, on the day when they about to partake of the Divine Sanctified Elements, not only before their communion, but also even after communion, the spouses ought to abstain. Those who do not do this shall be subject to austere penances.

Question 12

If a priest bathes, is he able to celebrate the liturgy on the same day? And a layman after going to the baths, may he be permitted on the same day to partake of the Mysteries? And contrariwise, shall the

---

41. Exod 19:10–11 (LXX).
42. Exod 19:14–15 (LXX).
43. Timotheos I, pope of Alexandria (d. 385), Question 5 (a paraphrase) (Rhallēs and Potlēs, 4:334).
44. Timotheos of Alexandria, Question 13 (Rhallēs and Potlēs, 4:338–339).

priest who celebrated liturgy or the layman who was deemed worthy of the Divine Sanctified Elements bathe or be bled, or not?

Response

Galen, the most learned among physicians, states, "Bathing, sun, and exercise put into motion the residues (τὰ περιττώματα) formerly at rest."[45] For which reason, nothing of which you asked shall take place. For also the incisions of veins control their evil properties, according to Hippocratic teachings, sometimes producing (κυΐσκουσαι) diaphoresis (διαφόρησιν), but more often at other times stoppage (στεγάνωσιν).[46] Indeed, why would we participate in the salvific communion of the Sanctified Elements in a manner expected probably to be evil, and easily overshadow the light of our salvation, where fitting reason compels the ones who perform sacred rites both before the sacred service and after the sacred service with all compunction and piety to bend their knees before God, and give thanks on account of partaking of the Lord's Body and Blood, and not to be enfeebled by slackness (βλακείας) and sprinklings of warm waters?[47] If a life-

---

45. Galenus Medicus (ca. 129–ca. 216), *De symptomatum causis* 2.5 (Kühn, 7.181.1). For an excellent overview of Galen's life, work, and influence, see Johnston. On the relationship of Galen to Hippocratic writings, see Brain, 112–121.

46. For στεγάνωσιν, the reading should most likely be στέγνωσιν. In Galenus Medicus, *De sanitate tuenda* 3.10 (Kühn, 6.218.13–14), στέγνωσις is defined as "τὴν βλάβην τῶν πόρων." In this case, the incision of the veins results in either a flow or stoppage of the residues from the pores. For a study of venesection in the thought of Galen, see Brain. Regarding the residues (τὰ περιττώματα) and overheating discussed, Brain states (Brain, 11):

> Galen, unlike some of the ancients whom he cites, postulated more than one mechanism for fever. The simplest variety, which he calls the ephemeral (though it may last longer than a day) is due simply to overheating of the body by the sun, anger, exertion, heat-producing foods or drinks, or to reduction of heat loss through insufficient transpiration when the pores of the skin are obstructed. Other fevers are the result of inflammation, with or without putrefaction. Both inflammation and putrefaction originate from residues, or perittomata, in the body, which are thus extremely important in Galen's pathology.

In this regard, bloodletting is used to eliminate the residues or prevent their accumulation (Brain, 13).

47. Eustathios of Thessaloniki (ca. 1115–1195/96), a contemporary of Balsamōn, terms bathing as a sign of slackness (βλακείας) (Tafel, 49, 228). While not making the connection to Balsamōn, Albrecht Berger provides an excellent discussion on Eustathios; see Berger, 67.

threatening illness impels the bloodletting, it shall be performed for
the salvation of the afflicted one.[48]

Question 13

If someone vomits after Holy Communion, by what tradition
might he be disciplined?

Response

It is written, "The one who observes holy things in holiness will
be holy and sanctified. The one who betrays grace will be polluted."[49]
If indeed the one who partook of the Divine Sanctified Elements
vomited from dissoluteness, he shall be corrected with more severe
penances. If from a distress because of an illness occurring by chance,
he shall be moderately penanced according to episcopal discretion,
for this is also a matter of dereliction.

Question 14

Shall one perform priestly functions or celebrate holy baptism on
a ship or in an unconsecrated house without danger?

Response

God said through Moses to Israel, "In Jerusalem and not in any
other place you shall celebrate the Pascha of the Lord your God,"[50] in
consequence clearly foreshadowing here the complete abrogation of
the Jewish Pascha, on account of the singularity of the place.[51] Canon

---

48. For a study of *alousia* or abstinence from cleansing in Byzantine canonical thought, see Viscuso, "Cleanliness." Although the translation of several
texts was thoroughly revised, additional research was added, and corrections
were made through the present work, these do not affect the main conclusions
drawn in the latter study on bathing prohibitions for clergy and laity.

49. Wisd of Sol 6:10 (LXX) (a paraphrase).

50. 4 Kgdms 23:19–23 (LXX) (a paraphrase).

51. The phrase "διὰ το τοῦ τόπου μονώτατον" was translated as "on account of
the singularity of the place." The word μονώτατον is derived from the superlative form of the adjective μόνος and is being used as an accusative substantive.
The root adjective μόνος is translated normally as "alone" or "only." When used
as an adjective, the superlative in its primary meaning can be translated as
"one above all others." As a substantive, it is likely being used to emphasize
the specificity of the place, in this case, of the location in Jerusalem of the
Judaic Paschal celebration. The translation "singularity" is meant to convey the
idea of "the exclusion of any other than" also associated with the meaning of
μόνος and reinforced by superlative use (see Muraoka, 467). In the response,
this singularity or specificity is viewed as a divine indication of the eventual
abrogation of the Jewish Passover by the Christian Pascha, which is not tied

59 of the Holy and Ecumenical Council that met in the Trullo of the Great Palace and canon 84 of the Council in Carthage subject to defrocking the one celebrating baptism in an oratory house. For they prescribed that baptisms take place in Catholic churches. However, canon 31 of the Council in Trullo, and canon 12 of the council held in the Temple of the Holy Apostles,[52] ruled that with episcopal permission baptisms are also celebrated in oratory houses. The celebrated emperor Lord Leōn the Wise, seeing the Orthodox faith flourishing like a vine and increasing as olive branches around the table of the churches decreed in his *Novels* 4 and 15, that sacred services and baptism might take place without distinction not only in churches

---

to a specific location. Underlying this point is likely the theological view of Christ as the new Passover Lamb (cf. 1 Cor 5:6–8) whose sacrifice is considered to have greater universal significance for human nature than the former Judaic practice, which is regarded as a foreshadow or prefigurement. These theological understandings, particularly emphasizing the former Jerusalem and its earthly restrictions, were established early in Eastern Christian tradition and expressed by the second century author Melito of Sardis in his *Peri Pascha* 45 (Hall, 23):

> The Jerusalem below was precious,
> but it is worthless now because of the Jerusalem above;
> the narrow inheritance was precious,
> but it is worthless now because of the widespread bounty.
> For it is not in one place nor in a little plot
> that the glory of God is established,
> but on all the ends of the inhabited earth
> his bounty overflows,
> and there the almighty God has made his dwelling
> through Christ Jesus;
> to whom be glory for ever. Amen.

The work is dated between 160–170 (Hall, xxii). Stuart George Hall analyzes the passage as follows:

> References to the temple and Jerusalem allude to the celebration of the paschal sacrifice, restricted in the Deuteronomic code to Jerusalem. They gain particular point from the cessation of the sacrifice when the temple was destroyed. Here the temple is taken as a model of the risen Christ, whose body it represents in John 2:19–21; cf. also Eph. 2:14–22.

52. First and Second (861), canon 12. Also called "First and Second," this council was held in 861 in the Church of the Holy Apostles in Constantinople and is regarded in the *Canonical Questions* as the Eighth Ecumenical Council. The circumstances of its convocation are summarized in Hartmann, 146–148. The council recognized Phōtios the Great as patriarch of Constantinople during his first reign (858–867).

but also in oratory houses.[53] For which reason, in accordance with their provisions, the one who celebrates sacred services with an *antimēnsion*[54] or baptizes in an oratory house that has not been consecrated through the dedicatory opening, the customary enthronement, and of course the entombment (ἐνσοριασμοῦ) of the holy relics (for these are treasures and exaltations of the Catholic churches), but which is designated for the household prayer of the faithful, or in a ship's cabin that is reserved for God and adorned with holy icons, might not be condemned as a transgressor of canons and slack. For so also the clergy who travel with the emperors have been correct to perform priestly functions in flat deserts, in only a silk tent set apart for a church.

Question 15
Shall one perform priestly rites or pray together without danger with heretics, namely Jacobites and Nestorians,[55] in their churches or

---

53. Leōn VI, the Wise, emperor (886–912), *Novels* 4 and 15 (Noailles, 21–25, 58–61).

54. According to Balsamōn, the *antimēnsion* is a type of portable altar blessed by a hierarch during the consecration of a church and used in place of an altar in a consecrated church in which relics are deposited. It is thus likely that the *antimēnsion* contained relics (cf. Izzo, 46–48). The canonist states in his commentary on Nicea (787), canon 7 (Rhallēs and Potlēs, 2:581–582),

One asked, "And how are oratories presently consecrated without the depositing of relics? And why are sacred services in them celebrated not by bishops, but priests alone?" And listen that the *antimēnsia*, which are created by hierarchs during the time in which a consecration of a temple takes place, when sent to oratory houses, suffice instead of a consecration or enthronement, dedication, and opening. For on account of this they were called *antimēnsia*, or substitutes (ἀντιπρόσωπα) and antitypes of many such tables (μίνσων, [mensae]), which furnish for the holy table of the Lord. Nevertheless, hierarchs do not celebrate sacred services in undedicated oratory temples, because the office of the archpriest is lowered when a throne does not readily exist on which the bishop is seated in an apostolic manner, nor the other things associated with the consecration and dignity of the temple.

55. *Jacobites* is a term derived from the name of Jacob Baradaios (Gk. Βαραδαῖος, Syr. Burd῾oyo), the sixth-century missionary and bishop of Edessa (542–578), who rejected the Christological teachings of the Fourth Ecumenical Council of Chalcedon (451) and adhered to those of Sebēros, patriarch of Antioch (512–518). The term is used here to identify his followers who originated in the environs of Edessa and later adherents. Sidney Griffith provides the following explanation regarding the use of the term (Griffith, 134–135):

When the emperor Justinian's policies subsequently forced public allegiance in Byzantium to the Chalcedonian Christological formula, those who followed the faith articulated by the long-deposed Patriarch Severus went underground. Their numbers and their perseverance were increased in the Syriac-speaking communities with the consecration of the sympathetic bishop Jacob Baradaeus (ca. 500–578), who was installed in Edessa in 542 at the behest of the leaders of the Ghassanid Arab tribal confederation who were important allies of Byzantine power on the Syrian and Arabian borders. Subsequently, due to the tireless clandestine activities of Bishop Jacob to support those who rejected Chalcedon and accepted the doctrine of the Patriarchs Cyril of Alexandria and Severus of Antioch, the whole community of them in the Syriac-speaking milieu came to be called Jacobites by their adversaries.

Griffith states that the community did not "consolidate their denominational identity with their own fully independent hierarchical structures" until under Arab government after the Islāmic conquests of the seventh century (Griffith, 135). In addition, the Copts, the dominant Christian community in Egypt during the twelfth century, were "often put together with the Jacobites in discussion of denominational differences" (Griffith, 137). Although sharing a common faith with Syriac-speaking Jacobites, the Copts preserved a separate communal and ecclesial identity in Egypt, and "had their own early Christian heritage both in their own language, Coptic, and in Greek, the dominant language of learning in the ancient patriarchate of Alexandria and the language in which St. Cyril of Alexandria, the principal theological authority for the Copts, wrote his letters and treatises" (Griffith, 136). However, from the tenth century on, the Copts adopted Arabic, like other Christian communities living under Islām.

Nestorians is a term derived from the name of Nestorios, bishop of Constantinople (428–431). According to Balsamōn, "Those who like Nestorios separate God the *Logos* and the humanity assumed by him are called Nestorians" (Rhallēs and Potlēs, 2:532). Balsamōn provides the following introduction to the Third Ecumenical Council (431) and explains Nestorios's theological views (ibid., 2:192):

> The Third Holy and Ecumenical Council took place under the reign of the emperor Theodosios the Younger, when two hundred fathers gathered in Ephesos, against Nestorios, patriarch of Constantinople, who said that Christ was a mere man, and taught that the Son of God was united with him by relationship. For which reason he dared to call the holy virgin not Theotokos, but Christotokos. He was defrocked and anathematized by the holy fathers.

According to Griffith, "The sociohistorical community lamentably misnamed Nestorian by their adversaries for polemical reasons had its origins not in Patriarch Nestorius's struggles with Patriarch Cyril in Byzantium, but in the Syriac-speaking, academic communities of Edessa and Nisibis in the days of the schoolman Narsai (d. 503) and Bishop Bar Sauma of Nisibis (d. before 496)" (Griffith, 131). These scholars of Edessa and Nisibis generated enthusiasm for Theodōros, bishop of Mopsuestia (392–ca. 428); Diodōros, bishop of Tarsos (378–d. ca. 394); and Nestorios, who came to dominate the theological

even our own, or might one share a common table with them, or perform sponsorship at holy baptism, or perform memorial services of
the departed, or commune of the Divine Sanctified Elements[56] with
them? For the area's difficulties create many such things, and I seek
what one must do.

Response

"Do not give holy things to the dogs," our Lord and God has said,
nor "cast pearls before swine."[57] Indeed, on this account canon 64 of
the holy apostles, the heralds of God, also states, "If any clergyman
or layman might enter an assembly of the Jews or heretics to pray, let
him be defrocked and excommunicated." Canon 33 of the Council in
Laodicea, but indeed also 6 and 34, states the following: "Concerning not permitting heretics to enter into a house of God while they
remain in heresy," because one must not pray with a heretic or schis-
matic, "a Christian must not abandon Christ's martyrs and depart
for false martyrs, namely, heretical ones or those that the aforementioned heretics produced. For these are estranged from God. Therefore, let those departing to them be anathematized." Indeed, on this
account we also decided that both clergy and laity are subject not
only to excommunication and defrocking when they pray together in
a church of Orthodox or heretics or whenever they pray together as
clergy, or even share a meal together, but also they shall be punished
in a more severe way, according to the provisions of the cited divine
canons. For the difficulties of areas, and the increase of heretics, did
not change the soundness of the Orthodox faith.

Question 16

Latin prisoners and others are present in our Catholic churches
and seek to partake of the Divine Sanctified Elements.[58] We seek to
learn whether this must indeed be permitted.

---

viewpoints of those who entered into "communion with the Church of the East,
whose patriarchal see was Seleucia/Ctesiphon in Persia" (ibid., 131). By the
sixth and seventh centuries, this community had developed its canonical and
ecclesial identity. Extensive theological works were produced in the succeeding
centuries in Arabic and Syriac. The Church of the East engaged in extensive
missionary work into southern Arabia, Iran, China, and southern India.

56. Holy Body and Blood of Christ.
57. Matt 7:6.
58. Holy Body and Blood of Christ.

Response

The Holy Gospel stated, "He who is not with me is against me, and he who does not gather with me scatters."[59] Therefore, since many years ago the formerly renowned assembly of the Western church (we speak of Rome) separated from the spiritual communion of the other four holy patriarchs, and things alien to the customs and dogmas of the Catholic Church and the Orthodox were excluded, for this reason, the pope is not deemed worthy of the general commemoration of names in the holy sacred rites. A member of the Latin nation ought not be sanctified by a priestly hand through the holy and undefiled Mysteries, unless he first promises to refrain from Latin dogmas and customs, is instructed in the canons, and is made equal to the Orthodox.[60]

---

59. Matt 12:30.

60. At the end of the eleventh century, crusader armies invaded the East. The Battle of Ḥaṭṭīn (1187) resulted in a critical crusader defeat by forces under the leadership of al-Nāṣir Ṣalāḥ al-Dīn Yūsuf ibn Ayyūb (1169–1193), the founder of the Ayyūbid dynasty in Egypt. The prisoners discussed were most likely crusaders captured during this period. The response reflects the Ecumenical Patriarchate's barring of Latins from the Eucharist prior to the taking of Constantinople by the crusaders of the Fourth Crusade in 1204. The main assumption of this response is that the Catholic Church consists of the communion of the four ancient patriarchates (Constantinople, Alexandria, Antioch, and Jerusalem), has holy and undefiled mysteries, and is Orthodox in faith. Latins are those who are part of the Western church under Rome, do not share in the communion of the Catholic Church, and have customs and dogmas alien to the Catholic Church. In light of these assumptions, the central problem raised by the question is whether Communion should be given to non-Catholics. The response provides reasons and conditions for barring from the Eucharist and conditions under which Westerners might receive Communion. They cannot receive while remaining Latins. Once they are made equal to Orthodox, that is, become Catholic, they can receive the Eucharist. While it is clear that Westerners must refrain from Latin dogmas and customs and be instructed in the canons in order to become Orthodox, the method by which they are received is not specified, that is, whether by baptism, anointing with *myron*, or confession of faith. Although not considered legislation of an ecumenical council and thus not regarded as having universal applicability, the guidance given in this response expressed the general approach to the question of intercommunion with Roman Catholics, which Orthodox churches maintain to the present. In contemporary ecclesial life, Roman Catholics are excluded from Communion until being made equal to the Orthodox (Viscuso, *Casebook*, 108).

Question 17

Is reception of the Divine Sanctified Elements self-chosen for all clerical and lay monks who have not been impeded, so that they would be able nearly every day to be sanctified through it, or is the Gift regulated as under a rule? But also for those of them who come to church, is reception of the Good Portion required, or chosen and self-bidden?[61]

Response

As it has been recognized, worthy things are given to the worthy, so also holy things to the holy (τοῖς ἁγίοις τὰ ἅγια).[62] Indeed, as many who by purity of life made the way of divine communion smooth for themselves shall receive freely, for they do not at all treat this casually, since they understand the sublimity of grace and the greatness of the Mystery. It has not been considered compulsory for them to partake of the Divine Sanctified Elements. For even if some, when referring to apostolic canon 9, which states the following: "All faithful entering and hearing the Scriptures who do not remain for prayer and Holy Communion must be excommunicated as ones who create disorder in the Church," desire that those who enter the church also involuntarily partake of the Divine Sanctified Elements, the content of the canon is not understood by us in this way. For we decided (ψηφιζόμεθα) that the faithful are to attend church until the end of the divine celebration, the last prayer of benediction, and the receiving of the *antidoron*,[63] and we threaten those who do not so do this with the rigor of the aforementioned canon, and we do not compel them to partake, because of pangs of conscience (διὰ τὴν τῆς συνειδήσεως βάσανον). Therefore, one must ensure, according to the content of the aforementioned canon, that those who attend church do not depart from the sacred worship in a disorderly way. But since the Old Testament and the New magnify this sacred worship in an identical manner, the psalms of the Davidic *kinnor* hallow the power of the Mystery also until the proclamation of the Holy Gospels. After

---

61. "Divine Sanctified Elements," "Gift," and "Good Portion" are the Holy Body and Blood of Christ.

62. The phrase "τοῖς ἁγίοις τὰ ἅγια" reflects the call to communion, "τὰ ἅγια τοῖς ἁγίοις," used in Byzantine Eucharistic liturgies. Both versions have the same meaning, "holy things for the holy." For the development of "τὰ ἅγια τοῖς ἁγίοις" as a call to communion, see Taft, *Precommunion*, 230–240.

63. Bread that is cut from the loaf used for the Eucharistic gifts and that is distributed at the conclusion of the service as a blessing.

this, the forecourts of the bloodless sacrifice are opened, which command the archpriests to take off the ōmophorion that is worn over the shoulders, beautifully fashioned in the form of a lamb, and celebrate the Mystery of the true and life-giving Lamb.[64] If those attending

---

64. This is a description of a liturgical action during the celebration of the divine liturgy. The ōmophorion was in its early development a non-liturgical vestment emblematic of the episcopal office as the image of Christ and of bishop's ministry as that of the Good Shepherd. This vestment was at first worn outside of the church and during processions, but gradually, by the twelfth century, became used during the divine liturgy with its removal just before the Gospel (Taft, "Omophorion"; Larin, 219–220). This usage is consistent with the Word service contained in a eleventh-century *diataxis*, or book of rubrics, for the pontifical liturgy of the Great Church, which states (translation from Taft, "Pontifical Liturgy 1," 291),

> After the blessing, when the archdeacon has said "Let us be attentive," the bishop says, "Peace to all," and then sits down. And while the psalmist is chanting the prokeimenon, after the end of the second verse, the archdeacon requests leave and the bishop, blessing him, says, "Blessed is our God, always, now . . ." And while the Apostle is being read, the deacon requests leave and a prayer for the one about to the read the Gospel. And he [the bishop], blessing him once, very slowly, for as long as it takes to complete the prayer of blessing, says in the hearing of the archdeacon: "May the Lord the King of Powers grant you speech for announcing the Gospel with great power, by the grace of his beloved < Son > always, now and ever, and unto ages of ages." After the exit of the Gospel, one of the seated bishops, having risen, goes to the first bishop and bowing, kisses [his] knee, and then bowing again, says, "Bless master." And [the first bishop] grants him leave to give the greeting of peace after the Apostle, saying, 'Blessed is our God, always . . ." But at the second verse of the alleluia the archdeacon also requests leave, saying, "Bless, master." And the bishop says, "Blessed is our God . . ." And he requests at the same time also the Prayer of Incense of the holy Gospel. And the bishop blesses the deacon who is facing the holy altar and showing the incense, saying "I offer incense . . ." While the last alleluia is being sung, the castrensis takes off the bishop's omophorion. And he stands and turns to the east and bows down his head to the throne for a short time until the archdeacon exclaims, "Wisdom, arise, let us listen to the holy Gospel."

For a summary of this vestment's history and usage, see Taft, "Omophorion"; Larin, 217–228; and Woodfin, 15–17. St. Isidore of Pelousion (d. ca. 435) is the first textual witness to the ōmophorion and states (PG 78:272, translation based on Taft, "Omophorion," 278),

> The ōmophorion, which the bishop wears on his shoulders, and is made of wool, not linen, signifies the skin of that lost sheep, which the Lord sought, and, having found, carried on his shoulders. For the bishop, who is the image (τύπον) of Christ, fulfills the latter's

church will freely depart immediately after the Holy Gospels, they shall not be reproached. However, if after the beginning of the bloodless and mystical sacrifice, they shall rightly be excommunicated as disorderly and offensive.

Question 18
Are deacons who concelebrate with an archpriest or priest necessarily obliged to partake of Communion, or not?

Response
Canon 8 of the holy apostles states as follows: "If any bishop, presbyter, deacon, or one on the list of clergy, when the offering is made does not partake, let him state the cause. And if it might be reasonable, let him be pardoned. But if he does not state it, let him be excommunicated, as one who becomes a cause of offense to the people, and causing a suspicion against the offerer, as one not offering in a fitting manner." Therefore, one must watch closely that the subdeacons, deacons, and much more, those receiving in their hands

---

work, and shows to all through the *schēma* that he is an imitator (μιμητής) of the Good and Great Shepherd who has been appointed to bear the weaknesses of the flock.

Regarding its removal during liturgical celebrations, see the following explanation in Woodfin, 19–20:

Another peculiarity of the bishop's vesting was his removal of the *omophorion* at the Gospel. This usage was apparently of great antiquity, attested as early as the fifth century. In the twelfth-century rubrics of the pontifical liturgy, the *kanstresios* is directed to take off the bishop's *omophorion* during the final alleluia before the Gospel and replace it upon his shoulders after the dismissal. The *Diataxis* of Gemistos supplies the further detail that the *kanstresios* carries the patriarch's *omophorion* in procession during the Great Entrance. In the later sources, the bishop resumes the *omophorion* at the elevation before distribution of communion. As with the wrapping of the deacon's *orarion* at the time of communion, the bishop's removal of his omophorion was interpreted as a gesture of humility. According to Kabasilas, the *omophorion* represents the bishop's authority. It is thus put aside for those parts of the service where he functions as a simple priest . . . In effect, when wearing the *omophorion*, the bishop acts as a stand-in for Christ, a role that is emphasized by the dignity in which he is vested in the sight of the people. The bishop's function as the image of Christ is effaced, according to the texts, through his removal of the *omophorion* in deference to the more perfect revelations of Christ in the Gospel and in the Eucharist.

(τοὺς χειραπτήσαντες), partake of the Divine Sanctified Elements,[65] or if not, state the reason for which they refrained from this good, because the ones not doing this shall be excommunicated according to the content of the aforementioned canon.

Question 19

Is it without danger for the administration and reception of the Divine Sanctified Elements[66] to take place with cold wine and water? Or is it necessary also for hot water to be placed into the Holy Things at the time of reception?

Response

When canon 32 of the Holy and Ecumenical Council held in the Trullo of the Great Palace subjected to deposition those who did not fill the divine and holy chalice with wine and water, certain heretics refused to put hot water into the holy and divine cup, because, they say, matters concerning this were not determined by the canon. However, understand that the hot water that is added to the Holy Blood does not change the union of the holy chalice by water and wine, since it is nothing other than water; and it is put forth in certainty that what flowed from the holy side of the Lord God and Savior Jesus Christ at the time of his salvific passion, that is, the blood and water, was life-giving, not dead, for while warm blood does not flow from a dead body, from the dominical body even after death blood and wine flowed warm as life-giving from a life-giving body that had been deified. At any rate, those who are not doing so, and who are not consequently magnifying the greatness of the miracle, but who are performing the communion of the Divine Mysteries[67] by using cold water and wine, do not believe that after the salvific death of the Lord the divine nature was in his holy body, but apostatize from this and believe that it was like our bodies, which is the prattle of a great heresy. For Iōannēs of Damaskos, who is great among the saints, states, "In the tomb with a body, in Hades with a soul as God, in paradise with a thief, and on the throne with the Father and Spirit, Christ, the uncircumscribed one filling all things."[68] At any rate, those who

---

65. Holy Body and Blood of Christ; in this context, τοὺς χειραπτήσαντες most likely refers to priests and bishops.
66. Holy Body and Blood of Christ.
67. Holy Body and Blood of Christ.
68. Paschal *troparion* attributed to St. Iōannēs of Damaskos (b. ca. 676– d. 749). The citation of this text may reflect a usage of the hymn during the

do not prepare the holy chalice with hot water shall be excluded as heretics from the portion of the Orthodox.[69]

Question 20

If one might let fall anything on the ground from the holy chalice or holy paten, what censure shall the one performing priestly functions in this case be placed under?

Response

Since "there is one glory of the sun, and another glory of the moon,"[70] there is also a distinction made among the Sanctified Elements allowed to fall upon the ground. For if any such blunder might take place before the Cherubic Hymn and before the placing of the holy chalice and holy paten on the holy table, an examination of the carelessness will be carried out and the matter shall be treated by a moderate penalty, because what falls is not reckoned to be the Lord's Body and Blood before the consecration of the Holy Elements, and the sanctification through them. However, if the evil occurred after the consecration and the completion of the Divine Mysteries, the Holy Elements shall be gathered with every honor, and the place on which they had fallen shall be given respect and scorched by fire and water. If the evil occurred because of his negligence, he shall be treated through more severe penance and deprived of exercising his office, but if because of demonic assault, he shall be punished moderately. For the involuntary sin also merits a canonical remedy, in order that the evil one might not appear to derive an advantage, blazingly pilfering the eternal from the one performing priestly functions.

Question 21

Is it allowed for an unordained monk, or even one who is ordained, to receive a confession from men on his own?

Response

The Lord said to the sacred divine heralds and holy apostles, "You are the salt of the world"[71] and "Whatever things you bind on earth

---

preparation of the Eucharistic gifts.

69. See Balsamōn's commentary on Trullo 32 (Rhallēs and Potlēs, 2:375–378) translated above in the notes to Question 1.

70. 1 Cor 15:41.

71. Matt 5:13.

shall be bound in heaven."[72] On account of which also our divine and holy fathers have prescribed canons, that the absolutions of confessions take place through the bishops, who are assigned an apostolic position from God. An ordained monk, even much more an unordained one, is not able to reconcile to God the one who confessed without permission of the bishop. Certainly all ordained monks shall receive confessions of men by episcopal permission (and to the unordained monk no episcopal favor bestows a faculty of absolution), remain unendangered themselves, and reconcile those who confess to God because canon 43 of the Council in Carthage clearly states the following concerning those who repent: "That to the repentant, in accordance with the distinction of sins, and by judgment of bishops, the time of repentance is fixed, and a presbyter does not absolve one who is repenting, unless forced by necessity in the absence of the bishop." And canon 7 of the same council states the following: "If anyone who is in danger requests for himself to be reconciled with the sacred altars when the bishop is absent, the presbyter should suitably ask the bishop, and so reconcile the one in danger according to his orders."

Question 22
Does a secular priest rightly undertake confessions of any men with episcopal permission, or not?

Response
The divine canons that assign to priests the confession of reconciliation with episcopal permission are much older than St. Pachomios, who was deemed worthy to see the *schēma* of monks by an angelic vision. [73] For this reason I suppose they have not mentioned monks, but simply priests. At any rate, through episcopal permission, the right of confession and reconciling through this those who repent can be legally entrusted to secular priests (τοῖς λαϊκοῖς ἱερεῦσιν).[74]

---

72. Matt 18:18.

73. St. Pachomios (ca. 290–346). The response reflects the tradition that the saint received a vision of an angel who presented him with a rule for the cenobitic monastic life, which became known as the *Rule of the Angel*. For an examination of the Pachomian tradition and its influence on Byzantine monasticism, see BMFD, 1:32–39.

74. The issue raised concerns over why monastic clergy are not mentioned as confessors in the canons. The canons in question appear to be those referenced in the preceding question, namely, canons 7 and 43 of the Council in Carthage. This response implies that these canons date earlier than the

Question 23

Is it without danger of condemnation that monks change to other monasteries from the monasteries where they were tonsured, or not?

Response

If one who makes his oath before men is compelled to fulfill this, how will the man making one before God not be compelled to keep his commitment inviolate? For this reason, and according to canon 4 of the Holy and Ecumenical Council held in the Temple of the Holy Apostles, the so-called First and Second,[75] which precisely states the following: "If any monk who runs away from his own monastery might change to another monastery, or might burst in upon a secular house, both he and the one who accepted him shall be excommunicated, until the deserter from the monastery that he wrongly left might return. However, if the bishop wishes to transfer some of the monks who are known for piety and chaste life to another monastery for establishment of the monastery, or chooses to establish them in a secular house for salvation of the inhabitants, or deems to place them elsewhere, this does not subject the monks or the ones who receive them liable to be tried." At any rate, those who change, against the will of the bishop, to other monasteries from the ones where they were tonsured, and much more those who reside in secular houses, and the ones receiving them, shall be cast out and deprived of Communion until they might return to the monasteries in which they had given their vows.

Question 24

Is it allowed for anyone to be a clergyman in different churches, or not?

---

development of monastic clergy, identified with St. Pachomios, who is credited traditionally with having established the oldest form of cenobitic monasticism. The term "secular priests" denotes parish clergy as opposed to hieromonks; cf. a similar usage in Balsamōn's commentary on the Nomokanōn in 14 Titles (Rhallēs and Potlēs, 1:41).

75. The "First and Second" was held in 861 in the Church of the Holy Apostles in Constantinople and is regarded in the Canonical Questions as the Eighth Ecumenical Council. The circumstances of its convocation are summarized in Hartmann, 146–148. The council recognized Phōtios the Great as patriarch of Constantinople during his first reign (858–867).

Response

The Lord said in the Gospels, "No one can serve two masters, for he will be devoted to the one and despise the other."[76] For which reason also canon 15 of the Seventh Holy and Ecumenical Council explains these things in detail word for word: "From the present time forward let no clergyman be assigned to two churches for this is characteristic of commerce and greed, and foreign to church custom. For we heard from the holy voice of the Lord itself that one cannot serve two masters, for either he will hate the one, and love the other, or will be devoted to the one and despise the other. Therefore, each one, in accordance with the apostolic voice, in whatever place he was called, there let him remain,[77] and serve in one church. For the things done in church matters on account of greed have become alien from God. There are various pursuits for the needs of this life. Therefore, let one provide for the needs of the body by them if one might wish. For the apostle said, 'These hands served for my necessities and for those with me.'"[78] Therefore, one must take care that the inviolable contents of this holy canon be observed strictly, for much neglect of it has taken place.

Question 25

An ancient custom prevailed in the land of Alexandria that deceased priests and hierarchs are anointed with holy *myron*[79] and buried. We seek to learn whether this is without danger of condemnation.

Response

It is an evangelical command that believers are baptized once in the name of the Father, Son, and Holy Spirit. Indeed, on this account, canon 47 of the holy apostles also states the following: "Let a bishop or presbyter, if he might baptize again one who has a true baptism, or does not baptize one who has been polluted by the impious, be defrocked as one who mocks the cross and death of the Lord, and who does not distinguish priests from pseudo-priests." Canon 18 of the Council in Carthage also prescribed the following: "If any

---

76. Matt 6:24; Luke 16:13.

77. 1 Cor 7:20 (a paraphrase).

78. Acts 20:34.

79. The oil of anointing employed for the sacrament or mystery of holy chrismation following holy baptism, the reception of converts as well as apostates, the consecration of holy altars, the deposit of holy relics, and other uses.

clergyman is ordained, he ought to remember to keep the laws that he give neither the Eucharist to the bodies of the deceased nor baptism." Indeed, those who anoint deceased priests, hierarchs, or any others with *myron* and prepare them for burial in this way are worthy of a great punishment, either as condemning the Orthodox who baptized them, or as not having complete assurance that they are communicants with the Orthodox, and condemning them before the final judgment.

Question 26

May the mutilated or one-eyed be deemed worthy of priestly rank, or shall the one who suffered illness after ordination also exercise the priesthood after the affliction, or not?

Response

And we said elsewhere that based on the Mosaic Law such ones are not advanced into the priesthood,[80] but canon 77 of the holy and all-praiseworthy apostles states the following: "If anyone has been afflicted with blindness in an eye or maimed in a leg, but is worthy of the episcopacy, let this take place. For mutilation of the body does not defile (μιαίνει) him, but pollution (μολυσμός) of the soul." And canon 78 of the same holy apostles so explains, "Let the deaf and blind man not become a bishop, not as one who has been defiled, but lest that church affairs not be hindered." Accordingly, all who

---

80. Lev 21:16–23 (LXX). The reference is likely to an unidentified decision of the Holy Synod. Balsamōn provides the following commentary on apostolic canons 77 and 78 (Rhallēs and Potlēs, 2:100–101):

Based on the Old Law, no one who had been mutilated in any part of the body was advanced into the priesthood. In addition, if after the priesthood he had any mutilation from sickness, he was impeded from the priesthood. The divine apostles decreed that those who are unable to exercise the duties of the priesthood not be accepted, but ordered that those able to exercise them, whether they are one-eyed or lame, are deemed worthy of ordination, for they [the apostles] desire that all have pure and unblemished souls, not bodies. If one becomes deaf or blind, or the body otherwise becomes sickly, shall he be removed from the priesthood in accordance with the Old Law? Solution: absolutely not. For it is uncompassionate and foreign to apostolic righteous judgment that he be judged as unworthy rather than worthy of mercy on account of the illness. And many hierarchs, priests, and deacons who were blinded, and otherwise gravely ill, and not able to exercise any hierarchical action, were not removed.

have been impeded by afflictions of illnesses from exercising rights of any priestly rank shall not be deemed worthy of ordination. However, those who so suffer badly after ordination are not prevented from exercising the priesthood on account of the illness, and thus being feeble, they exercise the priesthood unimpeded. For it seemed right to the divine heralds not to impede anyone from the priesthood on account of a mutilation of the body. However, if the wages of the sickness impede the office (τὸ σπούδασμα) of the priesthood, the one who is ailing shall be impeded from exercising (τῆς ἐνεργείας) it, but shall not be deprived of the honor. Rather, he shall be shown mercy, partake of the former honor, and also have the necessities of life, and so forth, according to earlier custom.

Question 27
Can a priest or deacon safely become a moneychanger, customs collector, physician, or astrologer, or not?

Response
Canon 6 of the holy and all-praiseworthy apostles states the following: "Let a bishop, presbyter, or deacon not undertake worldly cares; otherwise, let him be defrocked." Canon 81 also stated, "A bishop or presbyter must not lower himself into public offices, but attend to church needs. Therefore, either let him be persuaded not to do this or be defrocked. For no one can serve two lords, according to the Lord's command."[81] Canon 6 of the Council in Carthage directs "clergy not to obtain a living from a dishonorable or shameful pursuit."[82] Canon 10 of the same council directs clergy to be prepared for the teaching of children and reading of Scriptures, and not to be engrossed with worldly cares. Again also, a *prostagma*[83] of the celebrated lord Emperor Manouēl Komnēnos,[84] which was issued in November of the fifteenth indiction, for the admonition of certain clergy bankers, and inserted in the *sekreton* of the *oikeiaka*[85] in January of the fifteenth indiction, expressly orders the following: "My Majesty gives permission to all who purchased such moneychanging stalls to have commerce in these things in whatever place you find worthy and Roman persons. For it

---

81. Matt 6:24; Luke 16:13.
82. This appears to be the content of canon 16.
83. Administrative order.
84. Manouēl I Komnēnos, emperor (1143–1180).
85. The *sekreton* of the *oikeiaka* was a department of Byzantine government administration with fiscal responsibilities; see Jeffreys, 541–542, 550.

is not possible for you who are clergy to pursue such a profession, because you cannot be exempted due to fitting propriety on account of being clergy when you do something contrary to eparchial law. Therefore, let as many of you who, as it is mentioned, have acquired these things by purchase propose worthy persons to the eparch in order that he might receive them, and might certify them to be moneychangers instead of yourselves, freely, and without the customary practice also of payment of any kind."[86] Indeed, canon 36 of the Council in Laodicea states the following: "Priests or clergymen must not be sorcerers or enchanters, or mathematicians or astrologers, or make so-called amulets, which are prisons for their souls, and we commanded that those wearing them to be expelled from the Church." And chapter 22 of title 39 of book 60 states the following: "Geometry is publicly taught, but mathematics is condemned."[87] And the ancient law states, "Call ye mathematics astronomy."[88] At any rate, clergy who dare, and much more those of the *bēma*, to undertake performance of common work, whether to deal in governance and management of guilds (συστηματῶν), perhaps becoming moneychangers, or cloth merchants, or wine merchants, and astronomers, themselves shall be ordered to

---

86. Zepos, 1:416–417; Franz Dölger dates this *prostagma* to November 1151 or 1166 (Dölger, 1384):

> November 1151 or 1166 November—Προστάγμα (title) to a petition of clergy, who have acquired a banking business; the clergy should dispose of their business to anyone who is a respectable citizen; since they as clergy must not carry on exchange trade, also in their capacity, as clerical persons, they cannot incur the risk of violating provincial regulations (ἐπαρχικὸς ὁρισμός). Persons recommended by them are to be brought before the eparch, who shall issue them the exchange commission tax-free.

87. *Basilika* 60.39.23 (Scheltema, A8:3009); "Artem geometriae discere atque exerceri publice intersit; ars autem mathematica damnabilis interdicta est" (*Code* 9.18.2); for additional information on astrology within Byzantium, see Magdalino, *L'Orthodoxie*, and Evaggelatou-Notara. Flōrentia Evaggelatou-Notara believes that the association of mathematics and astrology was due to the use of calculations in observance of the stars (Evaggelatou-Notara, 448, n. 7 for bibliography) and that the eleventh century in particular was marked by an interest in mathematics, astronomy, and astrology, which in turn is reflected in the prohibitions contained in the canonical response, Balsamōn's letter cited below, as well as his commentary on canon 36 of the Council in Laodicea (Rhallēs and Potlēs, 3:205–206).

88. The citation of these legal texts is similar to that in Balsamōn's *Letter to the Most Honorable and Holy Metropolitan of Philippopolis concerning Not Reading a Mathematics Book* (Rhallēs and Potlēs, 4:512–513) and his commentary on canon 36 of the Council in Laodicea (Rhallēs and Potlēs, 3:206).

refrain from these uncanonical professions, and those who refuse shall be subject to defrocking. Although the art of physicians is determined among the wise to be capable of saving health, this does not take necessarily take place. "For the devices of men are precarious, and the diagnoses of many are miserable" (σφαλεραὶ γὰρ αἱ τῶν ἀνθρώπων ἐπίνοιαι καὶ τῶν πολλῶν διαγνώσεις δειλαὶ) according to ancient maxim.[89] At any rate, to what end might the clergyman, and much more the priest and the deacon, refrain from the ministry assigned to him, from the blameless and safe, and throw himself into often precarious and uncertain danger?[90]

---

89. This is similar to a portion of a speech on April 5, 1143, attributed by the Byzantine historian Nikētas Chōniatēs to Iōannēs II Komnēnos (emperor 1118–1143) after unsuccessful treatment of his wounds by physicians while on expedition: "σφαλεραὶ γὰρ αἱ τῶν ἀνθρώπων ἐπίνοιαι, ἡ δὲ τοῦ Κυρίου βουλὴ ἀνεπιποίητός τε καὶ ἀμετάπτωτος" (Chon 1:42), which is translated by Magoulias as "The designs of men are frustrated, but the Lord's will cannot be nullified and is immutable" (Magoulias, 24). On the other hand, the phrase used in the speech may also be a quotation of a well-known saying.

90. In his commentary on canon 6 of the Council in Carthage, Balsamōn states that a synodal decree issued in December of the sixth indiction of an unknown year during the reign of Loukas Chrysobergēs, patriarch of Constantinople (1157–1169/70), prohibited the practice of medicine by priests and deacons (Rhallēs and Potlēs, 3:344):

> But neither did he [Patriarch Loukas Chrysobergēs] allow priests or deacons to become senior physicians (ἀρχιητροὺς), stating that it is unacceptable for those who are handling the Holy Elements with phainolia [φαινολίων, "albs"] and sticharia [στιχαρίων, "tunics"] to put on secular clothing and to proceed forth with laymen, that is to say, with physicians.

Grumel lists the text of the decision as lost (Reg, 1092). Based on a review of canonical literature, the modern scholar Phaidōn Koukoules states, "It appears that this prohibition was generally not enforced" and in fact regards the response to Question 27 as evidence for continued medical practice by clergy (Koukoules, 6:1–12). Concerning the decree of Chrysobergēs, Koukoules observes that it also provides evidence for distinctive dress by Byzantine physicians during the period, dress that was also worn by clergy (Koukoules, 6:12, n. 7). Regarding medical practice during the twelfth century, see Magdalino, Empire, 361–366; and Grumel, "La profession." On attitudes toward physicians during the twelfth century, Alexander Kazhdan argues that at the end of the tenth century there existed a "lukewarm and negligent view towards medical doctors" and intellectuals did not consider them peers. However, a major change occurred in attitudes, and by the twelfth century "the physician enters as equal the establishment of functionaries and literati . . . He becomes respected, although mocked time and again" (Kazhdan, "The Image," 51); see

Question 28

A Monothelite[91] who has a priestly religious profession (ἐπάγγελμα) turned by repentance toward the Orthodox faith among us, and was received, and was sanctified. After a short time, returning to his own

---

also a similar argument repeated in Kazhdan, *Change*, 155–158. See also a brief discussion of the canonical response in Trōianos, "Ἰατρική," 477–481.

91. A heresy that taught that Christ had a single will and that was condemned by the Sixth Ecumenical Council (680–681). In seeking reconciliation with those who rejected the Christological teachings of Fourth Ecumenical Council of Chalcedon (451), the emperor Heraklios proclaimed this teaching in an edict known as the *Ekthesis* ("explanation" or "formula") of 638. The question's use of the term "Monothelite" does not refer to followers living during the time of Sergios I, patriarch of Constantinople (610–638), or Pyrrhos, patriarch of Constantinople (638–641, 654), who are associated with the seventh-century heresy. Rather, it is a "heresy category" that refers to followers in the sense of those who think similarly, and is used to apply the canonical tradition of the Church to contemporary circumstances. These categories provide a means of naming, differentiating, and classifying heresies. In doing so, heretics and heresies are placed in a taxonomy and described according to their nature (cf. Averil Cameron, *Heresiology*). The contemporary twelfth-century identity of "Monothelites" is not clear. It can be speculated that the subjects were the Maronites discussed above, members of a Syriac-speaking community prominent in the area of Syria/Palestine, which scholarly opinion believes represented a split among Chalcedonian Christians and held Monothelite doctrines. For a general overview, see Griffith, 139–140. Balsamōn provides the following description of Monothelite doctrine and its condemnation by the Sixth Ecumenical Council (Rhallēs and Potlēs, 2:293–294):

> The Sixth Council took place in this Queen of Cities when Kōnstantinos Pōgōnatos, father of Ioustinianos and a descendant of Herakleios, reigned as emperor. One hundred seventy holy fathers assembled against Theodōros, who was a bishop in Pharan; Honorius of Rome; Kyros of Alexandria; Sergios, Pyrrhos, Paulos, and Petros, who presided in the Church of Constantinople; Makarios of Antioch; Stephanos his disciple; and Polychronios, an elder of childish mind, who dared to teach that our Lord Jesus Christ has one will and one energy after the incarnation. They, along with those who thought the same, were excommunicated from the Church and anathematized by this holy council, which taught and confirmed that our Lord Jesus Christ has two natural wills and two likewise energies after the incarnation, not in a division of persons, but that not one nature of the two natures of Christ was unwilling or unenergetic, so that the characteristic properties of each nature are not done away with (I speak of energy and will), and the two natures, of which they are characteristic properties, do not appear combined.

vomit,[92] he became a heretic as before. And again, as he states, after being by himself, and perceiving the sin, he returned to the Orthodox faith, and was received, in the manner of the prodigal who rightly returned.[93] Since he also wishes even to be deemed worthy of the priesthood, we seek to learn what is to be done.

Response

The Holy Gospel states, "No one who puts his hand to the plow and turns back is fit for the Kingdom of God."[94] For which reason, in accordance with canon 14 of the Holy and Ecumenical Council in Nicea, which distinctly states here word for word, "Concerning catechumens who also lapsed, it seemed right to the holy and great council that after they spend only three years hearing, thereafter to pray with the catechumens," it is sufficient for one who so wickedly slipped, and who blew about here and there, to be received according to the text of the canon, for he shall not be deemed worthy of the priesthood.

Question 29

Can bishops, monks, and clergy become without danger heads of public offices and works, and persons charged with matters of governance, or not?

Response

The 630 holy fathers who assembled in Chalcedon, and who made the Fourth Council heavenly, wrote beautifully here in their canon 7 expressly concerning these matters: "We decreed that those who have once for all been enrolled into the clergy and who became monks neither enter the army or worldly rank; otherwise, that those who dare to do this, and who do not feel repentance so as to return to what they promised on God's account, be anathematized." And canon 83 of the holy apostles states the following: "Let the bishop, priest, or deacon who devotes himself to the military, who wishes to hold both a Roman office and a sacerdotal ministry, be defrocked. For the things of Caesar to Caesar and the things of God to God."[95] Therefore,

---

92. Prov 26:11 (LXX): "Just as when a dog comes upon his own vomit and becomes despicable, so is a fool when he turns back in his own wickedness to his own sin."

93. Luke 15:11–32.

94. Luke 9:62; the text quoted uses the word "turning" (στραφείς) rather than the "looking" (βλέπων) of the standard scriptural text.

95. The scriptural reference in the canon is to Matt 22:21.

the things decreed in such canons shall apply both to those monks
and others who are well governed in this way.

Question 30

A married couple chose the monastic life by perhaps a common
desire and allurement (ἀρέσκειαν) for profit of the soul. Since they are
living in one dwelling again, living together in every way and sharing
the same table, I seek to learn what to do in their case.

Response

The divine canons of the Holy and Ecumenical Council held in
the Temple of the Holy Apostles, the so-called First and Second,[96]
determined that tonsures take place in monasteries mandatorily,
and the vows of the tonsured are received by sponsors (ἀναδόχων).
Indeed, those not living in the monasteries where they changed
schēmas[97] and were tonsured, but in worldly dwelling places, shall be
threatened by the local bishop with excommunication and most severe penances so that they return rightly to where they left wickedly.

Question 31

If hierarchs who, when they ordain deacons and priests, but indeed also when they sanctify children of Orthodox through divine
baptism or even certain heretics, and likewise distribute the Divine
Sanctified Elements[98] to them, might require from them on account
of their efforts a certain amount of money, are they acting correctly,
or not?

Response

It is written, "Soldiers do not supply their own salaries."[99] And God
said through Moses, "You shall not muzzle an ox that threshes."[100] Indeed, if both the hierarch and priest that ordain or baptize seek to

---

96. First and Second, canons 2 and 5. The "First and Second" was held in
861 in the Church of the Holy Apostles in Constantinople and is regarded in
the *Canonical Questions* as the Eighth Ecumenical Council. The circumstances
of its convocation are summarized in Hartmann, 146–148. The council recognized Phōtios the Great as patriarch of Constantinople during his first reign
(858–867).

97. The word σχῆμα (*schēma*) can denote the outward appearance of a person and his or her status in life. Thus, in the case of monks, it can mean either
the habit proper or the monastic way of life.

98. Holy Body and Blood of Christ.

99. 1 Cor 9:7 (a paraphrase).

100. Deut 25:4 (LXX).

be supported by a moderate gift, and at the choice of the one who is ordained or otherwise sanctified, they do nothing improper, because it is customary for the one who ordains to be supported. If they do not seek such customary gifts, but heavy payments that also strain the capability of the one being ordained, they shall not just be attended to, but shall also be subject to defrocking. For canon 2 of the Fourth Holy and Ecumenical Council states, "If any bishop performs an ordination for money, and might reduce grace that cannot be sold to merchandise, and for money might ordain a bishop, presbyter, deacon, *chōrepiskopos*,[101] or any other of those enrolled in the clergy, or for money might nominate an *oikonomos, ekdikos, prosmonarios*,[102] or otherwise any of the canon (τοῦ κανόνος)[103] on account of dishonest gain, let him who attempted this, when found guilty, be put in danger regarding his own rank, and the one ordained profit nothing from the purchased ordination or nomination, but let him be deprived of the rank or office that he obtained through money. If anyone might be found mediating shameful and illicit expenses in this manner, let him be expelled from his rank if he might be a cleric, and let him be anathematized if he might be a layperson or monk." And canon 23 of the Holy and Ecumenical Council held in the Trullo of the Great Palace states the following: "Concerning that no bishop, presbyter, or deacon who distributes the undefiled Communion receive coin or anything whatsoever from the communicant, in exchange for such Communion. For neither is grace sold nor do we distribute the sanctification of the Spirit for money, but without guile it must be distributed to those worthy of the gift. If any of those enrolled in the clergy might be found requiring anything of any kind for which they distribute the undefiled Communion, let him be defrocked, as an emulator of the error and wickedness of Simon."[104]

---

101. The *chōrepiskopos* was ordained for a specific area of a diocese and did not have the right to ordain priests and deacons without the written permission of the bishop. For additional information, see Menevisoglou, 74–78.

102. For a discussion of these ecclesiastical offices within the fifth-century Church at the time of the Fourth Ecumenical Council (451), see Darrouzès, 11–50.

103. This refers to the list of clergy (*catalogo clericorum*).

104. Acts 8:9–24.

Question 32
Should those who come through recognition of the truth to the
Orthodox faith, namely, Nestorians, Armenians,[105] Jacobites, and
other heretics, be made perfect by holy *myron*[106] alone or also by divine baptism?

Response
Canon 95 of the Council in Trullo, which follows canon 7 of the
Second Holy and Ecumenical Council, distinctly states here word for
word, "According to the following order and custom, we receive those
who bring themselves to Orthodoxy and to the portion of those being saved from heresy. We receive Arians, Macedonians, Novatians
(who call themselves *Katharoi* and *Aristeroi*), and *Tessarakaidekatitai* or *Tetraditai*, as well as Apollinarians, when they give written
statements, anathematize every heresy that does not think as the
Holy, Catholic, and Apostolic Church of God thinks, and are sealed,
that is, are above all anointed with holy *myron* on the forehead, eyes,
nose, mouth, and ears. We say when sealing them, 'Seal of the gift of
the Holy Spirit.'[107] Concerning the Paulianists (Παυλιανισάντων) who

105. In the responses, Armenians were regarded as Monophysite heretics.
Concerning the Armenian community under Islām, Griffith summarizes
(Griffith, 137),
> The Armenians too, for the most part, have professed the same
> faith as the Jacobites while retaining their own independent hierar-
> chical structures and their own language and ecclesiastical litera-
> ture and cultural traditions. They have borrowed much from Syriac
> sources, but they have never adopted Arabic as a church language
> although they have lived in all parts of the Islamic world since the
> very beginnings of Islam and have long been fluent in Arabic for
> the purposes of everyday life. Also from the very beginnings of Is-
> lam there has been an important Armenian enclave in Jerusalem
> where they have persistently represented the Jacobite point of view
> in theological controversies . . . Interestingly, there is even some
> evidence that from the seventh century onward there was a group
> of Armenian Chalcedonians in Jerusalem engaged in theological
> activity and producing texts that had a considerable influence on
> ecclesiastical and political developments back home in Armenia.

106. The oil of anointing employed for the sacrament or mystery of holy
chrismation following holy baptism, the reception of converts as well as apostates, the consecration of holy altars, the deposit of holy relics, and other uses.

107. As in the case of Question 28, this question and response make use of
heresy categories. Regarding Arians, who were the followers of Arios (ca. 250–
336, a presbyter of Alexandria, condemned by the First Ecumenical Council in
325), Balsamōn states (Rhallēs and Potlēs, 2:114),

This Holy and First Ecumenical Council took place when Kōnstantinos the Great was emperor (in the second year of his reign), when 318 holy fathers gathered in Nicea of Bithynia, against Arios, who when he was a presbyter of the Church in Alexandria blasphemed against the Son of God, our Lord Jesus Christ, saying that he is not consubstantial with God and the Father, and is a creature; and there was a time when he was not. This holy council defrocked and anathematized him with his companions. It taught that the Son is consubstantial with the Father and true God, Master, and Lord, and creator of all created things, but not a creature, nor indeed a work.

Concerning Macedonians, who were the followers of Makedonios (d. ca. 362, a claimant to the see of Constantinople), Eunomians, and Apollinarians, Balsamōn provides the following explanation in his commentary on Second Ecumenical Council (381), canon 1 (Rhallēs and Potlēs, 2:167–169):

The present Holy Second Council had been gathered against Makedonios, and those believing similarly to him, who taught that the Holy Spirit is a creature and not God or consubstantial to the Father and Son, whom the present canon calls Semi-Arians, since they partly participated in the heresy of the Arians. For while the ones taught that the Son and the Spirit are creatures and of a different nature from the Father, the *Pneumatomachoi* thought in a healthy manner concerning the Son, but blasphemed that the Holy Spirit is created and alien from divinity. Those who themselves said that the Son and Holy Spirit are creatures were also called Semi-Arians. And they concluded that "we do not think that he became similar to the rest of the creatures, but in some other manner, and we say this, lest that passion might be thought attributed to the Father by generation," whereas they taught that the Word and the Spirit are not consubstantial (ὁμοούσιον) to the Father, but of like substance (ὁμοιούσιον). Through the present canon, this Second Council also confirmed the Orthodox faith proclaimed by the fathers at Nicea and declared every heresy to be anathematized, especially that of the Eunomians. Eunomios, who was a Galatian, bore the title bishop of Kyzikos, and he thought the same as Arios, indeed much worse, for he taught that the Son is mutable and a servant, and completely dissimilar to the Father. He also rebaptized those who agreed with his opinion, and when baptizing did one immersion by immersing them by the head, turning their feet up. And he foolishly said that the future punishment and Gehenna did not truly exist, but were threatening by fear alone. The same ones were also called *Eudoxianoi*, from Eudoxios, a fellow heretic with Eunomios, who after becoming bishop of Constantinople appointed Eunomios archpriest of Kyzikos. They are also named Anomoians, on account of saying that the Son and Spirit have no likeness by nature with the Father. The council also declared that the Sabellians were anathematized, they who were named from Sabellios the Libyan. He became bish-

op of Pentapolis of Ptolemy, and taught coalescing and confusion
when he combined and confounded the three hypostases of one
nature and divinity into one person, and one person having three
names represented in the Holy Trinity. He states the same one appears at one time as Father, at another time as Son, at another time
as Holy Spirit, transforming, and sometimes changing appearance.
Likewise, they also place under anathema the heresy of the Mar-
cellians, who are named from the heresiarch Markellos, who originated from Ankyra of Galatia, and became its bishop and taught
the same as Sabellios. But also they put the heresy of the Photinians
under anathema. They had their name from Phōtinos, who originated from Sirmium, was a bishop there, thought the same things
as Paul of Samosata, did not confess the Holy Trinity, and called
God only Spirit, creator of all things, and thought that the *logos*
is uttered and a divine command that renders service to God for
the creation of everything, as some mechanical instrument; and declared Christ to be a mere man who received the *logos* of God, not
by nature, but as uttered; and taught that he received the source of
his existence from Mary. And Paul the Samosatian talked frivolously
of many other things, and the Council in Ankyra defrocked him. In
addition to the rest, the council also condemns with anathema the
heresy of Apollinarios. Apollinarios was bishop of Laodicea in Syria,
and he clearly blasphemed concerning the economy, for he said that
the Son of God received a living body from the Holy Theotokos,
without a mind, since the divinity suffices in the place of a mind,
and being just as irrational as he thought the soul of the Lord to be,
so also said that he was not perfect man, and taught one nature in
the case of the Savior.

Balsamōn provides the following explanation of Novatians, *Katharoi*,
Aristeroi, *Tessarakaidekatitai* or *Tetraditai*, Apollinarians (4th–5th centuries),
Montanists or Phrygians, and Sabellians in his commentary on canon 7 of the
Second Ecumenical Council in 381 (Rhallēs and Potlēs, 2:189–190):

The canon separates heretics who enter the Church into two
types. And it states that some are anointed with *myron*, after first
anathematizing every heresy, and confessing to believe as the Holy
Church of God thinks, but it determines justly that the others
are to be baptized. And it said that the former, who ought to be
anointed only with *myron*, are Arians, Macedonians, Apollinarians,
and Novatians, which are called *Katharoi*, whose heresies we commented on in the first canon of the present Second Council. The
Novatians were also called *Sabbatianoi*, from a presbyter Sabbatios,
who observed the Sabbath like the Jews. The same are also called
Aristeroi, as ones who loath the left hand, and refuse to accept anything whatsoever with it. They are called *Tessareskaidekatitai* or
Tetraditai when they do not celebrate Pascha on a Sunday, but on
whatever day when the moon becomes fourteen days old, which is
most characteristic of the Jewish religion. The same are also called

afterward take refuge in the Catholic Church, a decision was set forth
that they are rebaptized without any doubt.[108] Eunomians, of course,

Tetraditai because when celebrating Pascha they do not break their
fast, but fast just as we do on Wednesdays (τὰς τετράδας). They do
this following the Jews. For after celebrating Pascha, they fast on all
seven days, eating azymes and bitter herbs, according to the regulation of the Old Law. [The canon] said that the ones who ought to
be rebaptized are Eunomians, who are baptized in one immersion,
and Monatanists, so called from a certain Montanos, who called
himself *Paraklete*, and through two low-class women, Maximilla
and Priskilla, uttered false prophecies. In addition to these also are
Sabellians, who are named thus from a certain Sabellios, who say
along with other silly things, the same one to be Father, the same
the Son, the same the Holy Spirit, as three names in one hypostasis;
as body, soul, and spirit in man; or as three energies, that is, the
form of a circle, the light, and the warmth, in a sun. The Montanists
are called Phrygians, either from a heresiarch Phrygos, or from the
fact that such a heresy first was seen from Phrygia. In addition to
these, *Pepouzianoi* are named from a certain land Pepouzas, which
is venerated among them like Jerusalem. Such ones dissolve marriages as abominable, observe a strange fast, pervert Pascha, reduce
and confuse the Holy Trinity into one person, and offer bread that
they make kneading together blood of a stabbed child with wheat-
meal. And so much for these things. If an Orthodox might become
a Montanist or Sabellian, and receives or does not receive a baptism
of heretics, shall such a man be anointed with *myron* or rebaptized,
as other Montanists? See canon 19 of the First Council and canon
47 of the holy apostles concerning this. Note from the present canon that all who are baptized in one immersion are baptized again.
    108. In his commentary on canon 19 of the First Ecumenical Council
(325), Balsamōn appears to confuse Παυλιανίσαντες, the followers of Paulos of
Samosata (third century), with members of a
later dualistic heresy, Παυλικιανοί (Rhallēs and Potlēs, 2:161):
    Concerning the Παυλιανισάντων, a question occurred regarding
    who they are, and while others said other things, I found in various
    books that the Manicheans took the name of Παυλικιανοί from a
    certain Paulos of Samosata, son of Manichean woman by the name
    of Kallinika. He was called a Samosatian, like one bearing the title
    of bishop of Samosata. He preached that there is one God, when
    saying Father, Son, and Holy Spirit were the same. For he says God
    is one and His Son is in him, as the *logos* in a man. This *logos* that
    came to earth lived in a man called Jesus, and fulfilling the econo-
    my, ascended to the Father. This Jesus from below is Jesus Christ,
    as one having his beginning from Mary. St. Grēgorios the Wonder-
    worker and certain others defrocked him in Antioch. There is still
    uncertainty whether Παυλιανίσαντες from Orthodox Christians ought
    to be rebaptized. And some say that the canon states that those who

who are baptized in one immersion; Montanists, here called Phrygians; Sabellians, who hold a belief in a doctrine of the identity of Son
and Father (υἱοπατορία) and commit some other abominable things;
and all the other heresies—because there are many here, especially
those that began from the land of the Galatians—all those of whom
wish to come to Orthodoxy, we receive as pagans; on the first day we
make them Christians, on the second, catechumens, then on the third
we exorcize them by breathing three times in the face and ears. And
thus we catechize and make them stay a long time in the Church to
listen to the Scriptures, and then we baptize them. We rebaptize the
Manicheans, Valentinians, Marcionists, and those coming from similar heresies, who are received as pagans. It is necessary for Nestorians,
Eutychians, and Sebērians to provide written statements and to anathematize their heresy as well as Nestorios,[109] Eutychēs,[110] Dioskoros,[111]
and Sebēros,[112] and the other exarchs of such heresies, those thinking
their things and all the aforementioned heresies, and in this way they
partake of Holy Communion." In any event, according to the text of
such a canon, some of the heretics are sanctified by baptism, and others perfected only by holy *myron*.[113]

---

are to be rebaptized are the ones who were Παυλικιανοὺς from birth,
not those who converted to the heresy of the Παυλικιανῶν from the
Orthodox, for those should be sanctified by *myron* alone.
For a brief discussion of the origins of the dualist sect, see L'Huillier, 81.
109. Nestorios, bishop of Constantinople (428–431).
110. Eutychēs, archimandrite of Constantinople (b. ca. 370–d. after 451).
111. Dioskoros, pope of Alexandria (444–451).
112. Sebēros, patriarch of Antioch (512–518).
113. Balsamōn explains his understanding of Manichees, Valentinians, Marcionists, and Nestorians (see also the notes on Question 15) in his commentary
on canon 95 of Trullo (Rhallēs and Potlēs, 2:531–532):
Concerning this canon, which is number 7 of the Second Council, we wrote sufficiently there and it is not necessary to repeat these
points again. Since it was added by this council that the Manichees,
Valentinians, Marcionists, and those from similar heresies, like the
Eunomians and Montanists, ought to be baptized, and Nestorians,
after giving written statements of their faith and anathematizing
Nestorios, Eutychēs, Dioskoros, Sebēros, and the rest who think
similarly to them, and their heresies, partake of Holy Communion.
Come, let us speak entirely concerning only these things. Well,
Manichees are those who think the things of Manēs, which Manēs
called himself *Paraklete*. He introduced that Christ appeared to be
suffering only by façade and [he introduced] two principles, evil and
good, that is, God and sun; slandered the Old Testament; turned toward worshipping the moon and stars as Gods; taught transmigra-

Question 33

If a heretical priest or deacon might be deemed worthy of divine
and holy baptism, or of sanctification by holy *myron*,[114] shall he serve
as a priest with his prior ordination, or might he be deemed worthy
of another ordination if he wishes to serve as a priest?

Response

Canon 80 of the holy apostles determined that those who came to
the Orthodox faith from the pagan life and were baptized are deemed
worthy of episcopal rank. Certainly, because the former priesthood is

---

tion of the souls; denied the resurrection of the flesh; and declared
plants, trees, and water to have rational souls. Valentinians are
Bogomils, Messalians, Euchites, and Enthusiasts found during the
time of Valentinos the Emperor. Marcionists originate from Marcion, the Marcion who spoke of three principles: first the invisible
God on high, second the visible creator and demiurge, and third
the devil. He baptized not only once, but also by a third immersion,
allowing women to baptize. Those who like Nestorios separate God
the *Logos* and the humanity assumed by him are called Nestorians,
concerning whom we wrote in the introduction of the Third Council. Likewise also concerning the heresy of Eutychēs, Dioskoros, and
Sebēros, we commented on similar matters in the introduction of
the Fourth Council. Therefore, read these things.
    Balsamōn considers the heresy of Eutychēs, Dioskoros, and Sebēros to be
identical and provides the following explanation of their teachings in his introduction to the Fourth Ecumenical Council (451) (Rhallēs and Potlēs, 2:216):
    The Fourth Holy and Ecumenical Council took place in the
time of the emperor Markianos, when 630 holy fathers gathered
in Chalcedon against Dioskoros, the renowned ruler over Alexandria, and Eutychēs, archimandrite of Constantinople, who while
confessing our Lord Jesus Christ to be consubstantial with the Father, blasphemed concerning the incarnation, and fell into another
evil diametrically opposite when fleeing the division of Nestorios,
who introduced two sons. For they impiously taught that the two
natures of divinity and humanity were commingled after the union
and were made into one nature, so also to attribute the passions to
the divinity. But they also said the Lord did not assume flesh consubstantial with us, nor composed from the Virgin's blood, but in
some unspoken, and more divine manner they imagined him to be
incarnate, and spoke foolishly of other things. This holy council
defrocked and anathematized them while teaching that our Lord
Jesus Christ is perfect man and perfect God, undivided and uncon-
fused in two natures. It set forth the canons that follow.
114. The oil of anointing employed for the sacrament or mystery of holy
chrismation following holy baptism, the reception of converts as well as apostates, the consecration of holy altars, the deposit of holy relics, and other uses.

considered an abominable ministry, and reckoned as not having taken place, if after being examined with canonical strictness the man who was once an abominable priest and thus became Orthodox might be found to be blameless regarding his former life, he might not only be deemed worthy of priestly but even of episcopal rank, after ascending completely through the customary ranks to the height of a teacher.

Question 34

If the wife and children of a man who came to the faith of the Orthodox from heresy, or even others related and sharing the same household with him, will not become Orthodox, but cling to the former heresy, shall the man perfected, as has been stated, through baptism, not be prohibited from ascending to priestly or episcopal rank? Or shall he also be deprived of such good on account of their evil?

Response

Canon 36 of the Council in Carthage states, "A bishop, priest, and deacon are not ordained before they make all those in their house Orthodox Christians." Canon 2 of the Holy and Ecumenical Council in Trullo determined in turn the following word for word:[115] "If certain ones who were still unbelievers, and not yet reckoned among the flock of Orthodox, were betrothed in legal marriage to one another, then the one who choose the good part joined with the light of the truth, and the other was restrained by the bonds of error, not choosing to gaze towards the divine rays, and the unbelieving wife agreed to live with the believing husband, or conversely the unbelieving husband to live with the believing wife, let them not be separated, according to the divine apostle: 'For the unbelieving husband is sanctified by the wife, or the unbelieving wife is sanctified by the husband.'"[116] Therefore, when canonically solving the apparent contradiction of these two canons, we say that (λέγομεν ὅτι) one who is Orthodox from birth and who joined himself with a heretical woman might not be deemed worthy of the clergy, unless he will also make those in his house Orthodox Christians, because he is one who has separated himself from the Church's assembly, so as to combine the sinful lot with the portion of Christ. If a man who was a member of a heresy from birth might choose the Orthodox faith, he shall rightly be deemed worthy of priestly ordination (if he is not impeded for

---

115. The correct reference should be to canon 72 of Trullo.
116. 1 Cor 7:14.

any other reason). The great apostle states, "For how do you know whether the faithful husband might lead his unbelieving wife to the faith?"[117] Therefore, the man who comes to the Orthodox faith from a heretical sect shall rightly be deemed worthy of priestly rank consistent with the canons, even if his wife and children do not become Orthodox.

Question 35
Is it without danger of condemnation for sponsorships of children to be performed by Latins, Armenians, Monothelites, Nestorians, and other such ones, or rather something hateful and to be averted?

Response
Paragraph 2 of chapter 18 of title 1 of book 1 of the *Basilika* states, "Indeed the man who turns a child from the Orthodox faith is heretical and subject to the laws against heretics."[118] Certainly, since all those enumerated in the present question were estranged from the Church of the Orthodox not by something small, but by a great and intricate divide, they shall by no means be joined in communion with us through sponsorship of spiritual children, which is mediated through many holy prayers and blessings, lest also we ourselves are condemned (κατακριθῶμεν) with excommunication according to the canon, which states, "The one who shares communion with the excommunicated is also excommunicated himself" (Ὁ κοινωνῶν ἀκοινωνήτῳ, καὶ αὐτὸς ἀκοινώνητος ἐστίν).[119]

---

117. 1 Cor 7:16 (a paraphrase).

118. *Basilika* 1.1.18.2 (Scheltema, A1:3); *Code* 1.5.2. Balsamōn's text is a paraphrase rather than an exact citation.

119. This phrase appears to be derived from the last section of the Council in Antioch, canon 2 ("If anyone of the bishops, presbyters, or deacons, or anyone of the canon [list of clergy] might appear to share communion with the excommunicated, this one also is to be excommunicated, as one who confuses the canon [order] of the Church," Rhallēs and Potlēs, 3:126) and is similar to texts from the synopsis of that canon attributed to the tenth-century Symeōn Metaphrastēs ("Καὶ ἀκοινωνήτῳ κοινωνῶν, ἔσται ἀκοινώνητος," Rhallēs and Potlēs, 3:129) as well as the commentary attributed to the mid-twelfth century canonist Alexios Aristēnos on the same legislation ("ὁ ἀκοινωνήτῳ κοινωνῶν, ἔσται ἀκοινώνητος," Rhallēs and Potlēs, 3:129). For a discussion of the authorship of the *Synopsis of the Canons*, see Hartmann, 120–124.

Question 36

Orthodox women are apparently joined in marriage with Saracens[120] or even with heretics and wish, like Orthodox as they assert, to partake of the Divine Sanctified Elements.[121] Therefore, we seek to learn what to do.

Response

Canon 72 of the Council in Trullo states the following: "An Orthodox man is not permitted to be joined with a heretical woman, nor is an Orthodox woman to be united with a heretical man. But if any such thing also appears to have been done by anyone, the marriage is considered null, and the illicit cohabitation is dissolved. For the mixable should not be mixed, nor the wolf combined with the sheep and the lot of sinners with the portion of Christ. However, if anyone would transgress the things decreed by us, let him be excommunicated." Indeed, how would she be deemed worthy of the Divine Sanctified Elements when she is cast out and excommunicated on account of this unlawful communion with a heretic? Absolutely not, unless she might cease from the evil, and be corrected through canonical penances.

Question 37

Some women who preside over female monasteries seek episcopal permission on account of hearing the confessions of the nuns under them. Therefore, we seek whether it is possible for this to take place.

Response

And we said at another time (καὶ ἄλλοτε εἴπομεν), the hearing of confessions is assigned only to priests with episcopal permission.[122] Certainly, if an unordained (ἀνίερος) abbot is not able to hear confessions with episcopal permission, much more is this not permitted to take place in the case of an abbess, even if her virtue might shine greater than the sun.

---

120. Muslims. The response may reflect the view of Islām as a Christian heresy articulated by St. Iōannēs of Damaskos (see the citation of texts in Griffith, 42).

121. Holy Body and Blood of Christ.

122. See Questions 21 and 22.

Question 38

The divine canons have made mention of deaconesses. Therefore, we seek to learn what is their ministry.

Response

Long ago orders of deaconesses were recognized by the canons,
and these also had a rank in the *bēma*. But the monthly distress[123]
excluded this service from the divine and holy *bēma*. Deaconesses
who do not have a participation in the *bēma*, but often attend church
services and maintain order in the women's part of the church consistent with ecclesiastical principles, are appointed by the most holy
Church and Throne of Constantinople.[124]

Question 39

Are deacons and subdeacons able to be legally united with wives,
or not?

Response

Various canons and laws prohibit clergy from being united with
a wife after ordination. Since such a canonical precept was being
violated, as it seems, the famous and wisest among emperors Lord
Leōn corrected the evil through an imperial constitution. For his
Novel 3 states in part the following word for word: "We order that
ordinations proceed according to the early and ancient rule of the
Church. For after being raised from bodily weakness by spiritual
ascent, it is not fit for them again to descend to bodily weakness.
On the contrary, the divine ministry must ascend from bodily weakness as a lofty ascension."[125] For this reason, no one of the *bēma* after
ordination might audaciously join himself to a wife according to a
law of marriage. Let the one who does this be defrocked, for it was
possible for him to do before ordination what was so wickedly dared
after ordination.

---

123. Menstruation.

124. This text provides evidence that by the eleventh century deaconesses
were no longer permitted in the *bēma* or altar as clergy, but were relegated to a
women's section of the Great Church, the Cathedral of St. Sophia, for the purpose of keeping order. For a study of Balsamōn's treatment of ritual defilement
and the prohibition of menstruating women from sacred space, see Viscuso,
"Images." A comprehensive and excellent study of women and sacred space in
Byzantium may be found in Taft, "Women."

125. Leōn VI the Wise, emperor (886–912), *Novel 3* (Noailles, 18–21).

Question 40

Is it permissible for priests who are abbots, or chief priests (πρωτοπαπάδας) and hierarchs, to be honored by *epimanika* and *epigonatia*, or has it been prohibited?[126]

Response

The most holy vestments of the *epimanika* and *epigonatia* have been bestowed only upon hierarchs, since they possess the image (τύπον) of our Lord, God, and Savior Jesus Christ and hence forgive sins of men, and do other greater things in imitation of Christ (χριστομιμήτως) that were not permitted for priests, for which reason they shall not be deemed worthy of either the *epimanika* or *epigontia*. For the *epimanika* is a representation of the fetters that were placed around the hands of our Lord, God, and Savior Jesus Christ when he was led to his voluntary passion, and the *epigonation* is a representation of the cloth with which the Lord toweled and washed the feet of the disciples. Therefore, just as the gifts bestowed upon patriarchs through vestments may not be given to any bishop, namely, the *sakkos*[127] and *polystaurion*[128] (for it has been deemed worthy for them to be honored by these things, as ones who are also commemorated to the ends of the *oikoumenē*[129]), so neither the privileges assigned to bishops shall be given to priests, lest a confusion of ecclesiastical

---

126. *Epimanika* were cuffs fastened over the sleeves of the *sticharion*, a tunic worn under other liturgical vestments such as the *sakkos*. During the twelfth century an *epigonation* was a square of stiff cloth suspended by a belt over the shoulder to the right knee. For an excellent discussion of the vestments addressed by Balsamōn, see Woodfin, 13–32; and Larin, 199–239, where their subsequent usage in Slavic churches is also treated.

127. A *sakkos* was a "dalmatic-like," T-shaped tunic. Balsamōn is credited as being the first witness to its liturgical use (Woodfin, 26).

128. The *polystaurion* is a *phelōnion* or cape decorated with a pattern of many crosses, which Woodfin dates as first appearing in art from the eleventh and early twelfth centuries, gradually gaining currency. Woodfin states (ibid., 23),

> The introduction of the *polystaurion* towards the end of the eleventh century is of critical importance, for it is the first vestment that differentiates its wearer not by the order of his sacramental ordination but by the rank of his see. Before the appearance of the *polystaurion*, it would have been impossible to differentiate by costume an image of a patriarch of Constantinople or Antioch from the bishop of a humble rural see.

129. The word *oikoumenē* has various meanings, which include the whole earth, the inhabited world, and the Roman Empire.

privileges takes place and the creation might say to the creator, "I am equal to you."

Question 41

By reason of an ancient indigenous custom, corpses of Orthodox are buried in our local churches. Therefore, I seek to learn whether this is without danger of condemnation.

Response

There is a great difference between churches that are consecrated through dedicatory openings and enthronement, chrism of holy *myron*,[130] and a deposit of holy relics of martyrs; and those not sanctified in this way and providing a place of prayer. For which reason, in the former in which the relics of martyrs have clearly been deposited, and in their midst you placed the chrism of holy *myron*, no human corpse of whatever kind shall be buried consistent with chapter 2 of title 1 of book 5 of the *Basilika*, which states, "Let no one bury dead in a church,"[131] and according to the old text in addition, which states, "It is not permitted to bury anyone in a church, if clearly the body of a martyr is laid in that place."[132] Corpses are buried without danger in those holy houses called oratories (εὐκτίους) that are not consecrated in this manner.[133]

Question 42

Inhabitants[134] (κατοικοί) of certain parishes (ἐνοριῶν) who requested ordination from their own hierarchs are approaching bishops of other parishes, and are ordained, as each one desires. I seek to learn if indeed this takes places safely for them.

---

130. The oil of anointing employed for the sacrament or mystery of holy chrismation following holy baptism, the reception of converts as well as apostates, the consecration of holy altars, the deposit of holy relics, and other uses.

131. *Basilika* 5.1.2 (Scheltema, A1:125).

132. This appears based on Ioustinianos, *Code* 1.2.2, "Nemo apostolorum vel martyrum sedem humandis corporibus existimet esse concessam" (cf. C. Th. 9.17.6).

133. For treatment of burial and death in general in the canonical thought of Balsamōn, see Viscuso, "Death."

134. Although an interpretative translation could be "members," the territorial nature of ecclesiastical organization implied by the word "inhabitants" would then be lost.

Response

The canons subject to the penance of excommunication readers who reject the ordinations of their bishops and who are deemed worthy of greater rank in other parishes through episcopal laying on of hands. And not only them, but also the ones who ordain them, just as matters concerning this are described by canon 54 of the Council in Carthage, which states the following word for word: "Clergy who belong to a church, as we already ruled, are not allowed to be appointed to a church of another city, but to be content with the one in which they were deemed worthy to serve from the beginning, with the exception of those who, when they lost their own native land, were transferred by necessity to another church. If a bishop, after this ordinance, receives a clergyman that belongs to another bishop, it seemed good that the one who receives and the one received are excommunicated, until the clergyman who moved might return to his own church."[135] Concerning the laity, it was once discussed by this Holy Synod of the Church of Constantinople, when the most holy and wise among patriarchs Lord Michaēl Anchialos (τοῦ Ἀγχιάλου) was patriarch.[136] A synodal decision (σημείωμα) took place during the month of November of the fourth indiction, which was composed from an assembly of various canons, that likewise determined both the layman ordained in another diocese contrary to the opinion of his bishop, and certainly the one who ordained him are punished.[137]

Question 43

Are deacons able to be deemed worthy of priestly rank contrary to the opinion of their archdeacon, or not?

Response

Providence concerning this has been bestowed upon bishops by the grace of the All-Holy Spirit because of which also, with their consent, deacons are made priests, while the archdeacon, as a confrere, only is present.

---

135. The contents of this canon address the same subject as canon 54 of the Council of Carthage in Rhallēs and Potlēs, 3:436–437, but the two texts are completely dissimilar.

136. Michaēl III, patriarch of Constantinople (1170–1178).

137. Michaēl III, σημείωμα συνοδικόν (Reg, 1118); cf. Rhallēs and Potlēs, 3:440–444.

Question 44

Shall laymen who married a second time be considered legally fit for another marriage, that is, a third one, or not?

Response

The old law regarded even third marriages as legal, and those born from it were heirs also subject to the paternal power. However, the canons of the divine and holy fathers not only do not recognize third marriage, but also even subject the second to moderate penance. Because when the celebrated emperor Lord Leōn the Wise[138] ruled, a great schism developed among the churches of the entire world, on account of the emperor not just marrying a third time but even marrying a fourth, a synodal assembly of nearly all of the hierarchs of the dioceses everywhere was held in the eighth indiction of the year 6428,[139] and which marital contracts ought to be averted and which permitted as legal were discussed when the celebrated emperor Kōnstantinos Porphyrogennētos[140] and his father-in-law Rōmanos[141] reigned. Indeed, after much controversy, and after careful examination, a synodal *tomos*[142] was drawn up, which was confirmed also by the customary signature of the emperor, that determined the fourth marriage to be abominable and not permitted, and the third to be partly permitted and partly not permitted. For it determined that men not yet forty years of age who had married a second time and were childless be permitted to contract a third marriage to remedy the childlessness, except that they be subject to penance for an entire five-year period, and so not receive the Divine Sanctified Elements.[143] After the five-year period, they receive Communion three times a year. But they [the divine fathers] permitted those who were thirty years old, on account of the weakness of their age, even if they had children, also a third marriage, obliging these men to be deprived of the Divine Sanctified Elements for a four-year period, thereafter and during future years to receive the Divine Mysteries[144] three times a year.

---

138. Leōn VI the Wise, emperor (886–912).
139. The year 6428, by Byzantine reckoning from the creation of the world, is equivalent to 920 AD.
140. Kōnstantinos VII Porphyrogennētos, emperor (908–959).
141. Rōmanos I Lekapēnos, emperor (920–944).
142. In this context, a *tomos* is an official document or decree.
143. Holy Body and Blood of Christ.
144. Holy Body and Blood of Christ.

The divine fathers ruled that by no means a third marriage be permitted for men over forty years of age. This *Tomos of Union* legislated these points. The Church did not forbid the contracting of a third marriage from then up to our times.[145]

Question 45

Is partaking of the Divine Sanctified Elements permitted for concubines, or not?

Response

Basileios, the great among hierarchs, did not give permission in his various canons for fornicators to receive the Divine Sanctified Elements.[146] It is determined in his canon 80 that the woman who fornicated, upon renouncing the fornication, does not receive the Divine Sanctified Elements at that point, but after three years.[147]

Question 46

Until what degree is the affinity (συμπενθερία) of co-parents an impediment?[148]

Response

Canon 53 of the holy and ecumenical council held in the Trullo of the Great Palace penalizes sponsors that unite in marriage with mothers of the children that were received from holy baptism, and after renunciation of the evil subjects them to the penance of fornicators. The last paragraph of chapter 10 of title 5 of book 28 of the

---

145. *Tomos of Union* (Reg, 715); for a critical edition of the *Tomos* with an English translation, see Westerink, 58–69; cf. Balsamōn's commentary on Basileios, canon 4 (Rhallēs and Potlēs, 4:103–107). The *Tomos of Union*, which formulated the decision of the local council of Constantinople in 920, resolved the Tetragamy Controversy, a conflict within the Church regarding the validity of the fourth marriage of Byzantine emperor Leōn VI (r. 886–912). The document also resolved questions of third and fourth marriage in general. In the *Tomos* the three times specifically named for communion of trigamists are Pascha, the Nativity, and the Dormition. In general, trigamists are otherwise not allowed to receive the Eucharist.

146. Holy Body and Blood of Christ.

147. Canon 80 concerns polygamy, not fornication, and imposes a penance of four years. Canon 59 deals with fornication, but imposes a penance of seven years.

148. The term "co-parent" (σύντεκνος) describes the relationship created between the godparent and the natural parent. Degrees of kinship are counted to determine impediments to marriage.

Basilika further lengthens the penalty.[149] Because also both the indicated canon and the above-named law state that spiritual kinship is greater than fleshly union, a synodal decision took place during the reign of that most holy patriarch Lord Nikolaos,[150] in the month of May of the fifteenth indiction,[151] over the question of that very honorable lord Grēgorios Xēros, which [synodal decision] determined that spiritual kinship established through co-parenthood is bound and falls under the same laws by which also kinships according to the flesh are regulated.[152]

Question 47

The land of the Alexandrians, which derives its ancestry from and is filled with countless numbers of Orthodox Christians, presently through divine dispensation is reduced by a moderate number of Orthodox Christians. Therefore, we seek to learn if it is permissible also for a marriage contract to take place within the sixth degree, on account of the necessity of the circumstances.

Response

The divine and sacred canons and laws, which are of the same mind in every way concerning marriage contracts, and which regulate marriage contracts with God-pleasing restrictions and teachings, do not permit these things to be violated in any way whatsoever. But they ruled that the marital union has been completely forbidden for ascendants and descendants and rightly restricted kinship of collateral relations up to the seventh degree and released kinship by affinity (ἐξ ἀγχιστείας), or συμπενθερία, after the sixth degree. Certainly the Alexandrians also ought to contract marriage in this way, and not put forward in justification of sin the reduction of Orthodox Christians, for the cohabitation that will take place in violation of these things shall be dissolved, and those who illicitly contracted shall be subject to the penances of fornicators. Since also by the *Tomos* of that most holy patriarch Lord Sisinios, two first cousins do not take two sisters in marriage, and the contract is reckoned in a sixth degree of

---

149. The cited section of the *Basilika* does not address spiritual kinship. Balsamōn is most likely referring to *Basilika* 28.5.15 (14) (Scheltema, A4:1348). Nevertheless, the latter does not specify a penalty.

150. Nikolaos III Grammatikos, patriarch of Constantinople (1084–1111).

151. 1092.

152. Nikolaos III, σημείωμα συνοδικόν (Reg, 964); cf. Balsamōn's commentary on Trullo, canon 53 (Rhallēs and Potlēs, 2:429–431).

affinity, be also knowledgeable on matters concerning this, lest in a spiritually harmful manner you might violate the Church's tradition by forgetfulness.[153]

Question 48

If a man might fornicate with a Christian woman prisoner, also Orthodox like him, shall he sell her as a slave without danger?

Response

The master shall have permission to sell his slave who was fornicated by him, and to profit from her purchase, for the slave who was fornicated by the master shall be deemed worthy of freedom when he mentioned nothing until his last breath concerning her sale taking place. For chapter 2 of title 19 of Book 48 states the following word for word: "If one might have a slave woman in a private union, not having a wife, and might remain with her until death, either having children from her, or not, and might not say anything concerning her in his will, she shall become free."[154]

Question 49

If an Orthodox might commit fornication with a Jewish or Hagarene[155] woman, might he be corrected through penance, or shall he be rebaptized?

Response

Canon 47 of the holy and all-praiseworthy apostles states the following: "Let a bishop or presbyter, if he might baptize again one who has a true baptism, or does not baptize one who has been polluted by the impious, be defrocked as one who mocks the cross and death of the Lord, and who does not distinguish priests from pseudo-priests." Perhaps one might then also say that an Orthodox man who committed fornication with an impious woman was defiled and ought to be rebaptized. However, this is not true because that man is defiled by

---

153. The *Tomos of Sisinios* was a synodal decree concerning marital impediments. It was issued in 997 by Sisinios II, patriarch of Constantinople (996–998). For additional information, see Reg, 804; for a text of the decree, see Rhallēs and Potlēs, 5:11–19.

154. *Basilika* 48.19.3 (Scheltema, A6:2250); *Code* 7.15.3.

155. A term used by Christian writers to refer to Muslims in general. The term is based on the name of Abraham's concubine Hagar (Genesis 16), who was viewed as the biblical ancestor of the Bedouin Arab Muslim invaders of the seventh century, and later became associated with Muslims in general (Griffith, 24, n. 6).

the impious when he willingly washes off divine and holy baptism and puts on a baptism of the impious. Certainly, according to episcopal discretion, he might be corrected through more severe penance both as a fornicator and as one who partakes of a satanic communion with impious ones, but he shall not be baptized.

Question 50
At what age might a man or woman be accepted for confession?

Response
The laws state that the sins of minors are pardoned. Minors are, in the case of males, those up to the fourteenth year, and in the case of females, the twelfth year. Perhaps then one might say that after their twelfth and fourteenth year of age, they ought to confess, since they are called to account for sins, and have become capable of fornication and certain other sins. However, it is our opinion based on experience of this, but also indeed on certain things that were stated in synods at various times concerning such matters, that both males and females ought to be corrected and sanctified through confession after the sixth year. Because also a clergyman who was engaged to a seven-year-old woman through written bonds, and after her death was joined to another woman, was not permitted by a synod to be canonically worthy of ordination, as a digamist, for the Holy Synod in Constantinople stated that a seven-year-old woman is capable of sexual desire, and consequently also is subject to corruption and being overcome by thoughts of fornication.[156] If these things have been rightly discussed in the case of a woman, they will much more be considered in the case of a man.

Question 51
If spouses might have fleshly relations during the night of the first day that bears the name of the Lord, shall they be penanced as those who act unlawfully, or not?

Response
And it has been stated above[157] that on Saturday and Sunday spouses ought to refrain from fleshly intercourse (τῆς σαρκικῆς κοινωνίας) on account of the spiritual sacrifice being offered to the Lord on these days, just as also Timotheos, patriarch of Alexandria,

---

156. Michaēl III, σημείωμα συνοδικόν (Reg, 1142).
157. See Question 11.

great among saints, replied to those who asked him concerning this.[158]
Indeed, how and when will those who do not live in chastity on these
days have leisure by common agreement (as the great apostle has
stated) for prayer and entreaty to God?[159] Never. For which reason,
those who so sin shall be corrected through moderate penances.

Question 52

If during the forty-day fast spouses did not live in chastity, shall
they be worthy of the Divine Sanctified Elements of Communion[160]
on the world-saving feast of Pascha, or not?

Response

If we have been taught not to eat fish and simply not to break
the fast throughout the whole holy forty-day period, and on every
Wednesday and Friday, much more shall they be required to refrain
from fleshly intercourse (τῆς σαρκικῆς συμπλοκῆς). Indeed, when
transgressing in this manner and transforming into satanic incontinence the salvific penitence springing from fasting and deliverance
from fleshly desires (as if the rest of the entire year did not suffice
them for the fulfillment of their fleshly desires), spouses shall not be
deemed worthy of Divine and Holy Communion on the feast day of
the Holy and Great Pascha, but will be corrected by penances.[161]

Question 53

Is it without danger on the day that bears the name of the Lord to
go to the baths and to cleanse oneself with warm water, or not?

Response

Both the divine fathers taught and *Novel* 54 of the emperor Lord
Leōn the Wise rightly legislated that the faithful refrain from any
work on the day that bears the Lord's name. For he states the following in part: "We also order, consistent with what was decided by the

---

158. Timotheos of Alexandria, Question 5 (Rhallēs and Potlēs, 4:334).
159. 1 Cor 7:5.
160. Holy Body and Blood of Christ.
161. Based on Questions 11, 51, and 52, marital relations are being associated with fasting. They are being associated with foods such as meats, animal-
derived products, and oil. Abstinence from certain foods and abstinence from
marital relations are being viewed as means of purification in order for the
clergy to intercede and mediate, and for both the laity as well as the clergy to
receive the Sacred. The appearance is being given that refraining from marital
relations is an attribute of purity and, when permanent in the form of celibacy,
perhaps also of a spiritual elite.

Holy Spirit and the apostles who were inspired by him, that all rest on the divine day dedicated to our immortality, and neither undertake farming nor any other work that is not permitted on this day. For if those who long ago honored shadows and types held the day of the Sabbath with such respect that they devoted themselves to complete rest, how equitable is it for those whom grace and truth make servants not to honor the day that the Lord enriched with dignity and freed us from the dishonor of corruption? Or, when one of the seven days is devoted to the honoring of the Lord, how is it not a complete lack of conscience for us not to be content with the six that are sufficient for work and to hold that one undiminished for the Lord, but to regard that day as a common one and to consider it a time for our own work?"[162] On account of which we also say (φαμεν καὶ ἡμεῖς) that all the activity of merchants and indeed farmers cease, as is stated, and all of them are compelled to be occupied in the churches, and rather to glorify God on this day that bears the name of the Lord, in order that on it we the faithful see the shining sun of righteousness. Therefore, the ones working the baths' furnaces, waters, and the rest shall neither serve them, nor might any faithful man be deemed worthy of pardon when abstaining from prayer, standing away from the greatly praised worship and teachings of the Lord's day, and being devoted and occupied with warm waters, but he shall be corrected according to episcopal discretion through penances.[163]

Question 54

Is the man who breaks his fast with meat, cheese, and eggs on Wednesdays and Fridays throughout the whole year pardonable, or not?

Response

Canon 69 of the holy apostles states, "If any bishop, presbyter, deacon, reader, or chanter does not fast during the Holy Lent of Pascha, Wednesday, or Friday, let him be defrocked, unless he might be prevented on account of sickness. If he might be a layman, let him

---

162. Leōn VI, *Novel* 54 (Noailles, 204–207).

163. Compare also Question 12. For a study of *alousia*, or abstinence from cleansing, in Byzantine canonical thought, see Viscuso, "Cleanliness." Although the translation of several texts was thoroughly revised, additional research added, and corrections made through the present work, these do not affect the main conclusions drawn in the latter study on bathing prohibitions for clergy and laity.

be excommunicated." Indeed, when a man without bodily sickness breaks his fast on Wednesdays and Fridays, he is punished according to the understanding of such a canon. When a man might be compelled to break his fast because of sickness, he shall alleviate the distress of the sickness with fish or oil, because he may not be permitted to avail himself of meat, cheese, or eggs either during Great Lent, or on any Wednesday or Friday whatsoever, even if he might be drawing his last breath. For it suffices for a man who ought by necessity to honor Wednesdays and Fridays with dry foods (ξηροφαφίας)[164] to deal reasonably with the disease by fish and oil. Exempted for me (μοι)[165] are Wednesdays and Fridays of meatfare,[166] cheesefare,[167] renewal week,[168] and the twelve-day feast,[169] for on these days we break our fast (καταλύομεν) without danger with meat because the Armenians fast during the twelve-day feast in honor of *Artzibourtzēn*,[170] from Monday during the week of meatfare, in honor of the Ninevites;[171] and the

---

164. Generally associated with bread and salt, but also uncooked vegetables and herbs, this type of fasting or abstinence not only concerned the type of food but also its preparation. For a general discussion, see Herbut, 32. From Balsamōn's commentary on apostolic canon 69, which is provided below, dry foods were required on Wednesdays and Fridays during Lent. Outside of the exceptions listed in the answer to Question 54, fasting on Wednesdays and Fridays during the rest of year required abstinence only from meat, dairy, eggs, and oil.

165. This is the only instance in the canonical responses where the first person is used.

166. Meatfare Sunday or week is the last part of the pre-Lenten liturgical cycle when meat is consumed, in preparation for the forty-day fast of Great Lent.

167. Cheesefare Sunday or week is the last part of the pre-Lenten liturgical cycle when dairy products are consumed, in preparation for the forty-day fast of Great Lent.

168. Easter week.

169. The twelve days associated with the celebration of the Nativity.

170. The Armenians were regarded as Monophysite heretics. In Byzantine polemical literature, *Artzibourtzēn* or *Artzibourion* was said to be the "favorite dog" of the Armenian teacher and holy man St. Sergios; see BMFD, 5:1679. Balsamōn appears to describe the Armenian Aŕaǰawor fast, a five-day fast that shifts on the liturgical calendar based on the Paschal cycle. The fast takes place three weeks before the Great Lent and ten weeks before Pascha. The reference to St. Sergios may be to the Armenian commemoration of St. Sargis Zōravar (a fourth-century martyr and military saint), which immediately follows but is not directly associated with the fast. For a discussion of this fast in medieval Armenian sources, see Renoux.

171. Jon 3:5 (LXX).

heretical *Tetraditai* observe a great fast during the week of cheese-fare.[172] Therefore, when acting in opposition to them, we break our fast lest we appear to share the same thinking with them; but this shall even take place when one shares the same table as *Tetraditai* and Armenians, for if such a man lives in a land where it is not possible to do this, he shall only take a taste of meat or cheese, and shall suspend suspicion with abstinence, not with gluttony. During renewal week we eat meat without danger on Wednesday and Friday, for this seven-day period is reckoned as one day named in honor of the Lord.[173]

---

172. For the *Tetraditai*, see Question 32.

173. The response is similar to Balsamōn's commentary on apostolic canon 69 (Rhallēs and Potlēs, 2:88–90):

> The forty-day fast of Pascha first was taught by the Lord, who fasted for such a number of days; and next through the present canon by the holy apostles, for they state, "If a layman does not fast during the Holy Lent of Pascha, and on every Wednesday and Friday (for also on these days in Holy Lent we equally ordered dry food to be eaten), if he is a clergyman, let him be defrocked, and if a layman, let him be excommunicated." Exempted for me are the sick, for those who break their fast with fish shall be pardoned. For one shall not break his fast with meat on any Wednesday and Friday whatsoever, except those of Pascha and the others allowed, even if he might be drawing his last breath. Exempted for me are the Wednesdays and Fridays of the week before meatfare and cheese-fare, and renewal week. For on these days we break our fast because the Armenians fast during the week before meatfare in honor of the Ninevites, and the heretical *Tetraditai* observe a great fast during the week of cheesefare. Renewal week is reckoned as Great Sunday itself; for this reason also morning resurrection Gospels are read every day. Likewise, exempted for me also are Saturdays and Sundays from the forty-day fast, for we break our fast similarly also on these, according to apostolic canon 66. When hearing "breaking fast," do not say with meat, for one is not permitted on account of bodily illness, even if he might be drawing his last breath, to eat meat during Great Lent. At various times we see that this is examined in synods, and not permitted.
>
> Note from the present canon that properly speaking there is one fast, the forty-day, that of Pascha. For if there were others, the canon would have also mentioned them. Except we are not ashamed when also fasting during other days of abstinence, that is, of the holy apostles, the Dormition of the Holy Theotokos, and Nativity. Read also what we wrote on the third question of synodal responses that took place during the days of the patriarch Lord Nikolaos.

Question 55

Are the fasts of the feasts of the Holy Apostles, the Nativity of Christ, the Dormition of the Holy Theotokos, and the Savior[174] required, or optional and unimportant?

Response

The Holy Synod in Constantinople during the days of that most holy patriarch Nikolaos, when asked if it is necessary to keep the fast in August, answered that this fast was changed to avoid falling on heathen fast days that take place during this time, and besides many men still fast this fast.[175] After examining matters concerning

---

174. The feast of the Holy Transfiguration.

175. Nikolaos III Grammatikos, patriarch of Constantinople (1084–1111). The reference is to responses made by the Holy Synod dated ca. 1105 (Reg, 982), which appear in manuscripts under the title *Questions of certain monks practicing asceticism outside of the city and answers made to them by the Holy Synod, during the days of the most holy patriarch Nikolaos, when the emperor lord Alexios Komnēnos of pious memory reigned, upon which also commentaries were written by the patriarch of Antioch Theodōros Balsamōn* (Rhallēs and Potlēs, 4:417–426). The third question deals with the necessity of fasting in August, and the answer is accurately summarized by the response above. Balsamōn's commentary repeats the point that seven days of fasting precede the feasts of the Holy Apostles, the Nativity of Christ, the Transfiguration, and the Dormition (Rhallēs and Potlēs, 4:419–421):

Question 3

If it is necessary to keep the fast in August.

Response

The fast was earlier in this season and was changed in order to avoid falling on heathen fast days that take place during this time, and besides many men still fast this fast.

Commentary. The question concerning this fast was once examined before our mighty and holy emperor in the presence of that most holy patriarch Lord Loukas and attending hierarchs. And some said that we ought not to fast on account of the change shown in the answer, but others objected that since the Holy Synod undoubtedly states that fasting did not take place formerly on these days, and this was changed, and it is not known how and where the change took place, we ought by necessity to fast. The patriarch and hierarchs decided that fasting is required during the month of August, and in establishing their reason they consulted also the *Tomos of Union*, which states that trigamists partake of the Divine Sanctified Elements three times during the year, clearly on the Great Pascha, on the feast of the Dormition of the Most Holy Theotokos, and on the Nativity of our Lord Jesus Christ, because of the fast that precedes these days and the benefit from this. When some still then doubted, on account of not finding anywhere decreed the amount

this, we (ἡμεῖς) answer (ἀπολογούμεθα) that by necessity fasts precede

of days of such a fast, the most holy patriarch himself said that since
the number of days of both this fast and that kept before the Nativity of Christ are not known from any writing, we are compelled to
follow unwritten ecclesiastical tradition, and ought to fast from the
first day of the month of August, and from the fourteenth of the
month of November. If we are compelled to break our fast on account of bodily illness, the known days of fasting shall be reduced
with episcopal permission, because this has also been established
by unwritten ecclesiastical tradition. And these things were said
then. After examining where and how these two fasts were handed
down, that is, that of the Dormition of the Holy Theotokos and that
of the Nativity of Christ and our God, but also the fast kept before
the feast of the Holy Apostles, and the fast before the Transfiguration, and whether we ought by necessity to fast during these times,
and for how many days, I state that the fast of four such feasts is required, but the amount of its days is not absolutely the same number
as it is for Great Lent, but all the faithful, clearly laity and monks,
are compelled to fast by necessity seven days before each of these
feasts, and those not so doing shall be excluded from the communion of Orthodox Christians. Monks who are compelled by founders' *typika* to fast additionally, that is, from the feast of All Saints,
and from the fourteenth of the month of November, involuntarily
shall also be compelled to follow the their founders' *typika* because
this is canonical and salvific, just as also laity who voluntarily fast in
this way shall be deemed worthy of praise. Since we confirmed the
causes of all these things in divine scriptural dogmas and teachings
pleasing to God, and presented them through a letter written to the
most honored monk Lord Theodosios the Sarpeiōpēs, who confines
himself on the Mountain of St. Auxentios, read also this, for here
it was not covered in as many lines. The same letter was written in
precisely the same way also to the clergy and laity in the throne of
the Great Antioch.

At its outset, the commentary makes mention of the decision of the Holy
Synod under Loukas Chrysobergēs, patriarch of Constantinople (1157–
1169/70) (Reg, 1089), and the *Tomos of Union* dated July 9, 920, which was
directed toward the settlement of the Tetragamy Controversy and stipulated
that the communion of third-married was allowed following major fasting
periods on the feast days of Pascha, the Dormition, and the Nativity (Reg, 715).
The commentary also makes reference to Balsamōn's letter to the Antiochians
concerning fasting, which in turn also notes the responses under Nikolaos III
(Rhallēs and Potlēs, 4:567). The letter appears under the title *Letter of the most
holy patriarch of Antioch lord Theodōros Balsamōn, concerning the fasting that
ought to be practiced each year, which was sent to the Antiochians*, in Rhallēs
and Potlēs, 4:565–579. For an overview of Balsamōn's commentary and letter,
see Stevens, 99–101. An extensive discussion concerning the regulation of
fasting in Byzantine monastic foundation documents may be found in BMFD,

these four feasts, indeed before the feast of the Holy Apostles, the Nativity of Christ, the Transfiguration of our Christ and God, and the Dormition of the Holy Theotokos, albeit seven days, for there is one forty-day fast, the fast of the Holy and Great Pascha.[176] If one fasts for more than seven days for the feast of the Holy Apostles, and for the feast of the Nativity of Christ, either willingly or when one is compelled by a founder's *typikon*, he shall not be ashamed.[177] How and why before each of these four feasts we ought by necessity to keep a seven-day fast was shown in the synodal *tomos* that we issued concerning this.[178] Indeed, those who do not fast before each of these four feasts according to everything that is required shall be corrected through great penances.

5:1696–1716. For the development of fasting practices in general within Byzantium, see Herbut.

176. Balsamōn discusses the length of the fast for Pascha extensively in his commentary on apostolic canon 69 (Rhallēs and Potlēs, 2:88–89); see its translation in the notes to Response 54.

177. This parallels Balsamōn's observations in his commentary on the third question discussed above as well as in his letter on fasting, where he states that the monks and inhabitants of Constantinople observe a fast from the feast day of All Saints until that of the Holy Apostles and forty days before the Nativity based on the influence of monastic regulations in *typika*, but maintain seven-day fasts for the Transfiguration and Dormition (Rhallēs and Potlēs, 4:577):

> Because in the Queen of Cities those in monastic life and the majority of her inhabitants maintain a brief fast after the feast of All Saints until the feast of the Holy and All-Laudable Apostles, even if it is not always forty days (which is influenced by the solar cycle, now one way lengthened, and another shortened), but also fast a forty-day fast before the Nativity of Christ and God, when following the *typika* in question, and by the grace of God also advance the affairs of holy churches to a more holy condition, you also ought to fast in this manner. Celebrate deliberately and necessarily the remaining two feasts, that is, the Transfiguration and the Dormition of the Holy Theotokos, with a seven-day fast.

178. The reference is most likely not to the decision of the Holy Synod under Loukas Chrysobergēs, cited by Balsamōn at the outset of his commentary on the third canonical question discussed above (Rhallēs and Potlēs, 4:417), which did not address the feasts of the Transfiguration and Holy Apostles and provided for longer fasting periods than seven days. Balsamōn's letter on fasting is not a *tomos* and moreover was issued in his capacity as patriarch of Antioch. It is possible that the reference may be to a lost act of the Holy Synod under Geōrgios II Xiphilinos, which issued the canonical responses to Patriarch Markos III.

Question 56

Shall those who abstain during these fasts, and in addition also those who eat dry foods on Wednesdays and Fridays, be given a second meal to care for bodily need, or not?

Response

Abstinence (ἐγρατεία) is properly fasting (νηστεία), because the one who kills the passions (παθοκτόνος) is not called one who kills men (ἀνθρωποκτόνος). Indeed, if those who abstain might eat also a second meal for sustenance of the body, they shall not be punished, for assuredly they do not dishonor the whole day's abstinence by evening incontinence, but let those doing the latter be penanced.

Question 57

On the eve before the feast of the Raising from the Dead of the Righteous Lazaros, and on a feast of saints during Lent, shall one celebrate a Divine Liturgy without danger, or not? Likewise also during the entire holy forty-day fast, is it possible to baptize, or to perform benedictions of marriages and betrothals, or not?

Response

Canon 52 of the holy and ecumenical council that met in the Trullo of the Great Palace states the following: "On every fast day of Holy Lent, except Saturday, Sunday, and the holy day of the Annunciation, let the Sacred Liturgy of the Presanctified Gifts take place." And canon 49 of the Council in Laodicea states the following: "That during Lent bread must not be offered, except on Saturday and Sunday only." And canon 51 of the same council states, "That births of martyrs must not be celebrated during Lent, but to make commemorations of holy martyrs on Saturdays and Sundays." And canon 52 says, "That one must not celebrate marriages or birthdays during Lent." Canon 45 of the same council states, "That after the second week of Lent one must not receive those for illumination." Indeed, those who contrary to the understanding of these matters celebrate baptisms or marriage benedictions during all of Holy Lent, or celebrate divine liturgies, except only on Saturday, Sunday, and the Annunciation, violate the law (παρανομοῦσι), and shall be corrected by great penances, as those who sin unpardonably. Of course on Great Saturday it has been ruled by the canons that baptisms take place. If loss of life compels celebration of divine baptism, baptism shall take place also on another day of Lent, because even for those who are penanced to the utmost extent, and condemned to absolute excommunication, the mystery of death helps for partaking of the Holy Mysteries.

Question 58

Do ordinations of subdeacons, deacons, priests, and hierarchs take place during holy and Great Lent without danger, or not?

Response

It has been ruled by the canons (just as it has been stated above) that the full celebration of sacred rites (τελείαν ἱεροτελεστίαν)[179] does not take place during the entire Lenten fast, except on Saturdays, Sundays, and the feast of the Annunciation alone. For which reason, during these days, when also the Mystical Sacrifice[180] that has been perfected is celebrated, ordinations shall take place, completely without condemnation. On the remaining fast days, when the full celebration of sacred rites does not take place, nor shall an ordination be celebrated of any of those of the *bēma*, much more an episcopal one. For ordination is also a time of festivity and glorification of God, which bestows spiritual honors to the worthy.

Question 59

Shall things of any kind or even fruits offered by anyone in the holy churches of God be received and held under authority by someone? And what and which are the ecclesiastical taxes (κανονικά) given annually to priests and hierarchs?

Response

The gold and silver vessels and utensils brought before God are not possessed, even if bishops offer them to God. It has been ruled by the canons that the fruits and drink customarily carried into the temple on anniversaries of saints and memorial services for the departed, and the things offered to the churches by anyone as donations benefiting the soul (ψυκικῶν διαδόσεων), are given to the bishops, and

---

179. In this context, the "full celebration of the sacred rites" refers to the full Divine Liturgy as opposed to the Liturgy of the Presanctified Gifts, which lacks the celebration of the Eucharist ("the Mystical Sacrifice that has been perfected"); involves the distribution of elements previously sanctified at a full Divine Liturgy; and appears to have a somber character, hence the additional reason that ordinations do not take place, since they involve festivity in the bestowal of honors to those worthy of clerical rank.

180. The Eucharist.

distributed by them to the clergy and to brethren under hospitality and otherwise destitute, according to their discretion. For canon 3 of the holy apostles states the following word for word: "If any bishop or priest might offer any other things for sacrifice on the altar contrary to the Lord's command, whether honey, milk, artificially strong drink instead of wine, birds, any animals, or vegetables contrary to law, let him be defrocked, except for new wheat, in due season. Let it not be permitted to bring anything else to the altar except only oil for the lamp and incense at the time of the holy oblation." Let all other fruit be sent home, first fruits to the bishop and presbyters, but not for the altar. It is clear that the bishop and presbyters make the distribution to the deacons and the remaining clergy.[181] And canons 7 and 8 of the Council in Gangra order the following: "If anyone might wish to receive offerings, or to give them outside of the church, contrary to the opinion of the bishop, or when he has been entrusted with such things, might not wish to do something with his approval, let him be anathema." "If anyone might give or receive offerings except the bishop or the one who has been appointed as steward of alms, let the one who gives and receives be anathema." And apostolic canon 2 states the following: "If a clergyman or layman takes for himself wax or wine from the holy church, let him be excommunicated."[182] And canon 73 states, "Let no one appropriate for his own use a consecrated gold or silver vessel, or linen, for this is a unlawful. If anyone might be discovered doing this, let him be subject to excommunication." Canon 10 of the holy and ecumenical council held in the Temple of the Holy Apostles subjects to defrocking those who use the things of the *bēma* as secular property, excommunicates those who convert sacred vessels for an unsacred use outside of the *bēma*, and condemns those seizing them as sacrilegious.[183] Kyrillos the Great in his letter to Domnos states the following: "Each of us will have to give account of his own affairs to the Judge of all. For it is necessary for valuables and real property to be preserved unsold for the churches, and the management of expenses when they arise to be entrusted

---

181. These are the contents of apostolic canon 4.

182. These are the contents of apostolic canon 72.

183. Also called "First and Second," this council was held in 861 in the Church of the Holy Apostles in Constantinople and is regarded in the *Canonical Questions* as the Eighth Ecumenical Council. The circumstances of its convocation are summarized in Hartmann, 146–148. The council recognized Phōtios the Great as patriarch of Constantinople during his first reign (858–867).

to those who preside over the divine priesthood at the time."[184] See also book 54, title 3, chapter 2.[185] The canons do not determine anything concerning how much ought to be given for an ecclesiastical tax by the commoners (κοινολαϊτῶν). A *prostagma* of the celebrated emperor Lord Isaakios Komnēnos prescribes, "Many things are given to the bishops by the laity who are assigned to their dioceses. Since irregularity and deficiency concealed the state of these things (for a small number of them do not give anything to the bishop), we are satisfied with the custom and conduct of those who give."[186]

Question 60

An Orthodox who, when he was taken prisoner by the Hagarenes,[187] also under force renounced the Orthodox faith and was circumcised almost all the time mourns over the impurity, and secretly meets with the Orthodox, and is reclaiming his salvation. Since he also wishes to partake of the Sanctified Elements,[188] we seek to learn what to do.

Response

Crowns are for those who struggle. And our Lord and God Jesus Christ said, "If anyone will confess me before men, I also will confess him before my Father who is in heaven."[189] Indeed, an impure vessel for reception of *myron* will be accepted by a deranged man.[190] For which reason the one repenting in this way and wishing to undergo a change for the good shall be deemed worthy of the consolation of episcopal and other spiritual instruction but shall not be deemed worthy of the Holy Mysteries. For first he ought to be cleansed of the pollution of impiety and then be received; and after the customary time he shall also become a sharer of Holy Communion.

---

184. St. Kyrillos of Alexandria (378–444), canon 2.

185. *Basilika* 54.3.2 (Scheltema, A7:2485). The title in question deals with the assignment of civic responsibilities and does not appear relevant to the discussion. It is likely that the reference is incorrect.

186. Isaakios Komnēnos, emperor (1057–1059), *Prostagma* (Dölger, 943; cf. Rhallēs and Potlēs, 1:75).

187. Muslims.

188. Holy Body and Blood of Christ.

189. Matt 10:32.

190. The oil of anointing employed for the sacrament or mystery of holy chrismation following holy baptism, the reception of converts as well as apostates, the consecration of holy altars, the deposit of holy relics, and other uses.

Question 61

A mob of peasants present me with one who appears to them to be worthy of episcopal or priestly rank and implacably demand that he be confirmed and ordained a hierarch or deacon. Therefore, I seek to learn whether we are compelled to comply with the cries of the crowds.

Response

Formerly, the ordinations of bishops and other clergy took place by the voting of the crowds and those who had influence with them. Canon 13 of the Council in Laodicea, and canon 3 of the Seventh Holy and Ecumenical Council, banished such ordinations from the institution of the Church. For the former states, "Concerning not permitting crowds to hold elections of candidates to be appointed to clerical office." The latter states the following: "Let every election that took place by the archons, of a bishop, presbyter, or deacon, remain invalid, according to the canon that states, 'If any bishop who, when making use of secular powers, through them comes to have possession of a church, let him be defrocked and excommunicated, and all who have communion with him.'[191] For the one about to be advanced to the episcopacy must be chosen by bishops just as also was decreed by the holy fathers of Nicea, in the canon that states, 'It is indeed fitting for a bishop to be appointed by all of the bishops in the eparchy, but if this might be difficult either on account of urgent necessity or length of travel, when at least three meet together at the same place, and those absent vote with them and express themselves in writing, the ordination is performed. The validity of what takes place is confirmed by the metropolitan in each eparchy.'"[192]

Question 62

Shall children born from a second marriage, slave women, and concubines be deemed worthy of the priesthood, or not?

Response

Children of a second marriage are not impeded by any reason from becoming clergy. For the synodal *tomos* issued during the reign of the emperor Lord Kōnstantinos Porphyrogennētos made the second mar-

---

191. Apostolic canon 30.
192. Nicea (325), canon 4.

riage equal to the first in all things,[193] on account of which also they are heirs subject to paternal power. But even those children born from slaves and who were given freedom, likewise also those born from concubines, shall not be impeded from becoming clergy. For their mothers fell under the penances for fornicators, but the children did not sin, and on this account are not subject to penances. Indeed, for the rest of men who have not committed sin, they also shall be deemed worthy of the honorable priesthood according to the canons.

Question 63

A reader who was entrusted by an abbot to manage monastery properties wishes to preside over priests who are there and other clergy, and to be commemorated with the abbot in the sacred services. Accordingly, I ask to learn whether he is asserting himself in a good way concerning this.

Response

Order holds the heavens and things of the earth together. For which reason also our Lord Jesus Christ, who repulsed the vanity of vainglory, said, "When you are invited to a marriage by someone, do not be reclining on the chief place, but go to the last place so that you will hear from the one who had invited you, 'Friend, go up higher'; in this way there will be much glory for you."[194] Indeed, the reader who seeks to be seated before the priests and to be commemorated with the abbot thinks in a manner contrary to the Lord's commands. However, if according to your narrative the reader dwells in the country while acting in place of an abbot, he strives rather worthily without danger to be placed before the priests and be commemorated, as one holding the place of him who entrusted the function to him. And this is supported by canon 7 of the Holy and Ecumenical Sixth Council held in the Trullo of the Great Palace, which states the following in part: "We have learned that in some of the churches certain deacons, who have audaciousness and independence, dare to seat themselves before the presbyters . . . unless when acting in the name of his own patriarch or metropolitan, he

---

193. This refers to the *Tomos of Union* dated July 9, 920, which was directed toward the settlement of the Tetragamy Controversy (Reg, 715). For a critical edition of the *Tomos*, see Westerink, 58–69; cf. Balsamōn's commentary on Basileios 4 (Rhallēs and Potlēs, 4:103–107).
194. Luke 14:10.

comes to another city on some question, for then he shall be honored as one who acts in place of the latter."[195]

Question 64

If a rural priest might perform a benediction of a third marriage,
while knowing that it was a third marriage, may he be punished, or
as a peasant shall he be deemed worthy of pardon?

Response

The one ignorant of the fact, whoever he may be, is worthy of
pardon in accordance with the laws. The one who is ignorant of the
law is not pardoned. Since by the new legislation of the celebrated
emperor Lord Kōnstantinos Porphyrogennētos,[196] the third marriage
is sometimes permitted, and sometimes not permitted (for those
who have children from the first or second marriage, and those who
exceed forty years of age, are not able to contract a third union), we
say (φαμέν) that the priest who had performed a benediction of such
an impeded third marriage is to be defrocked, because he was ignorant of the law's main points. However, peasants, who are ignorant of
the law's fine points, are pardoned sometimes, since legal matters are
not clear to all men.

Question 65

A woman who was being forced by her own father to be legally
joined with a husband, and upon seeing the union being guaranteed
by her father through written contracts, sent word of the marriage
taking place to a man who was erotically attracted to her. The good-
for-nothing man, as one maddened by love, arrived one evening at
the house of the woman with some of his low-class companions and
abducted her willingly, and brought her back to his house, which
is situated in the area of another village. Therefore, I ask to learn
whether those who so organized such abduction can be joined canonically through a benediction. For the parents of the woman also
wish presently for this to take place.

Response

Chapter 3 of title 58 of book 60 of the *Basilika* states the following word for word: "Let not the abducted woman be married to him
that abducted her, but if her parents also agree to such a cohabita-

---

195. The text is freely excerpted.
196. *Tomos of Union.*

tion, they are deported."[197] And canon 27 of the Holy and Ecumenical Fourth Council states the following: "The Holy Council determined that those who abduct women under the pretense of marriage, and accomplices or accessories of the abductors, if they might be clergy, shall be expelled from their rank, and if laity, shall be anathematized." For which reason also, when following both legally and canonically what has been so legislated, we say (ἡμεῖς ... λέγομεν) that if the points of the case have so occurred just as the question presented, neither shall a marriage take place between the abducted woman and the abductor, even if her father approves what took place; nor shall those who connived in this avoid the penances for abduction, but they shall also be punished to the utmost.

Question 66
A wife who fell seriously ill threw herself into the sea during an evening hour and drank the cup of death apparently in order to relieve herself from the suffering of the disease. Therefore, her husband, who is a reader, both then and at present asked whether he is henceforth impeded from priestly rank.

---

197. *Basilika* 60.58.4 (Scheltema, A8:3112); cf. Ioustinianos, *Novel* 143. Angeliki Laiou's analysis was helpful in clarifying the translation in question (Laiou, "Sex," 137). With regard to this response, Laiou provides the following analysis (Laiou, "Sex," 137–138):

> Balsamon's answer is uncompromising: they may not marry according to the provisions of Bas. 60.58.1 [sic], which also states that the parents, if they agree to the marriage, are to be exiled. Furthermore, the abductor and his accomplices shall be anathematized, according to the provisions of canon 27 of the Council of Chalcedon. Thus the consent of the woman does not at all alleviate the penalty, as indeed it does not in formal civil law, but she herself is not punished. And yet this case has all the elements of elopement: the girl wishes to marry a man and the abduction is only a feint, presumably to protect her reputation; the parents' hand is forced, as it often is in such cases; in the end, all the relevant parties want the marriage. It might be thought that Balsamon objected to the marriage because the girl was already engaged, but he does not at all mention this in his argumentation and, since the engagement was a civil one, not an ecclesiastical one, he perhaps did not find it binding in this respect. His objections, therefore, are on the formalistic grounds that this was abduction, and the civil laws absolutely forbade marriages resulting from abduction.

Response

If the points of the case occurred in accordance with your narrative, the reader shall be ordained without any impediment. For since the negligence of the careless person does not hinder the serious one, in accordance with the provisions of the divine laws, neither shall the fall of his wife punish the reader. For each is tied to his or her own cords, according to the saying.

Appendix 1

CANONICAL SOURCES

The Canons of the Holy Apostles

4th century	Attributed apostolic authority	Originated in Syria

Ecumenical Councils

325	First Ecumenical Council	Nicea
381	Second Ecumenical Council	Constantinople
431	Third Ecumenical Council	Ephesos
451	Fourth Ecumenical Council	Chalcedon
553	Fifth Ecumenical Council	Constantinople
680–681	Sixth Ecumenical Council "The Holy and Ecumenical Council held in the Trullo[1] of the Great Palace"	Constantinople
691–692	"The Holy and Ecumenical Sixth Council held in the Trullo of the Great Palace"[2]	Constantinople
787	Seventh Ecumenical Council	Nicea
861	"The Holy and Ecumenical Council held in the Temple of the Holy Apostles, the so-called First and Second"[3]	First and Second Constantinople
879–880	"The Holy and Ecumenical Council held in the most holy cathedral of Constantinople"[4]	Holy Wisdom Constantinople

Local Councils

251	Carthage
314	Ankyra
315	Neocaesarea
Ca. 340	Gangra
341	Antioch
Between 343 and 381	Laodicea
343	Sardica
394	Constantinople
419	Carthage

Holy Fathers

St. Dionysios of Alexandria, the Great	d. 264/265, r. 247/8–264/5
St. Grēgorios of Neocaesarea, the Wonderworker	b. ca. 213–d. ca. 270
St. Petros of Alexandria, the Martyr	d. 311, r. 300–311
St. Athanasios of Alexandria, the Great	b. 295, r. 328–373
St. Basileios of Caesarea, the Great	b. 330–d. 379
St. Timotheos of Alexandria	d. 385
St. Grēgorios the Theologian	b. 329/330–d. ca. 390
St. Grēgorios of Nyssa	b. 335/340–d. after 394
St. Amphilochios of Ikonion	b. 340/345–d. after 394
St. Theophilos of Alexandria	b. ca. 345–d. 412
St. Kyrillos of Alexandria	b. 378–d. 444, r. 412–444
St. Gennadios of Constantinople	r. 458–471
St. Iōannēs of Constantinople, the Faster	r. 582–595
St. Tarasios of Constantinople	r. 784–806
St. Nikēphoros of Constantinople, the Confessor	r. 806–815

Imperial Issuances Cited in the *Canonical Questions*

Leōn VI, the Wise, emperor (886–912)	*Novel 3*	Noailles, 18–21	Question 39
Leōn VI, the Wise, emperor (886–912)	*Novel 4*	Noailles, 21–25	Question 14
Leōn VI, the Wise, emperor (886–912)	*Novel 15*	Noailles, 58–61	Question 14
Leōn VI, the Wise, emperor (886–912)	*Novel 54*	Noailles, 204–207	Question 53
Isaakios Komnēnos, emperor (1057–1059)	Prostagma	Rhallēs and Potlēs, 1:75; Dölger, 943	Question 59
Alexios I Komnēnos, emperor (1081–1118)	*Novel 24*	Zepos, 1:305–309; Dölger, 1116	Questions 8, 9
Manouēl I Komnēnos, emperor (1143–1180)	Prostagma	Zepos, 1:416–417; Dölger, 1384	Question 27

References to the Basilika in the *Canonical Questions*

Basilika 1.1.18.2	Scheltema, A1:3	Question 35
Basilika 2.1.41	Scheltema, A1:19	Question 1
Basilika 2.4.21	Scheltema, A1:71	Question 4
Basilika 28.5.15 (14)	Scheltema, A4:1348	Question 46
Basilika 46.3.1	Scheltema, A6:2124	Question 3
Basilika 46.3.5	Scheltema, A6:2125	Question 3
Basilika 48.19.3	Scheltema, A6:2250	Question 48
Basilika 54.3.2	Scheltema, A7:2485	Question 59
Basilika 60.39.23	Scheltema, A8:3009	Question 27
Basilika 60.58.4	Scheltema, A8:3112	Question 65

Ecclesiastical Legislation Cited in the *Canonical Questions*

Nikolaos I Mystikos, patriarch of Constantinople (901–907, 912–925); Local Council of Constantinople (920)	*Tomos of Union*	Westerink, 58–69; Reg, 715	Questions 44, 62, 64
Sisinios II, patriarch of Constantinople (996–998)	*Tomos of Sisinios*	Rhallēs and Potlēs, 5:11–19; Reg, 804	Question 47
Nikolaos III Grammatikos, patriarch of Constantinople (1084–1111)	σημείωμα συνοδικόν	Rhallēs and Potlēs, 2:429–431; Reg, 964	Question 46
Nikolaos III Grammatikos, patriarch of Constantinople (1084–1111)	Questions of certain monks . . .	Rhallēs and Potlēs, 4:417–426; Reg, 982	Question 55
Michaēl III, patriarch of Constantinople (1170–1178)	σημείωμα συνοδικόν	Rhallēs and Potlēs, 3:440–444; Reg, 1118	Question 42
Michaēl III, patriarch of Constantinople (1170–1178)	σημείωμα συνοδικόν	Reg, 1142	Question 50

1. In the Canonical Questions the Council in Trullo is considered an extension of the Sixth Ecumenical Council. It was held in 691–692 and called "in Trullo" since its assembly was held under the dome (τροῦλλος) of the great imperial palace in Constantinople. In the Canonical Questions the council is not associated with the Fifth Ecumenical Council or *called by the name* Πενθέκτη (*"Fifth-sixth"*), even though the fathers of Trullo in their address (Προσφωνητικὸς λόγος) to Ioustinianos II Rhinotmētos, emperor (685–695, 705–711), considered themselves as completing the work of the previous two ecumenical councils by promulgating canons (Rhallēs and Potlēs, 2:298). See the analysis of Heinz Ohme in Hartmann, 77–84; and for an Orthodox perspective on the ecumenicity of Trullo, see Durǎ. According to Nicolae Durǎ, Balsamōn was the first to use the term Πενθέκτη ("Fifth-sixth") as a title for this council in his commentaries based on the understanding that Trullo supplemented what was lacking in the two previous ecumenical councils (Rhallēs and Potlēs, 2:300). A text of its canons based on the edition of Joannou is reproduced with an English translation in Nedungatt, 43–186.

2. Question 63.

3. Questions 14, 23, 30, and 59.

4. Question 9.

Appendix 2

Historical Persons Named in the Canonical Questions

Patriarchs of Constantinople (Reign Dates)

Sisinios	996–998
Nikolaos III Grammatikos	1084–1111
Michaēl III	1170–1178
Geōrgios II Xiphilinos	1191–1198

Byzantine Emperors (Reign Dates)

Leōn VI, the Wise	886–912
Kōnstantinos VII Porphyrogennētos	908–959
Rōmanos I Lekapēnos	920–944
Isaakios Komnēnos	1057–1059
Alexios I Komnēnos	1081–1118
Iōannēs II Komnēnos	1118–1143
Manouēl I Komnēnos	1143–1180
Isaakios II Angelos	1185–1195, 1203–1204

Other Ecclesiastical Figures

St. Pachomios	b. ca. 290–d. 346
Nestorios, bishop of Constantinople	r. 428–431
Dioskoros, pope of Alexandria	r. 444–451
Eutychēs, archimandrite of Constantinople	b. ca. 370–d. after 451
Sebēros, patriarch of Antioch	r. 512–518
St. Iōannēs of Damaskos	b. ca. 676–d. 749
Markos III, patriarch of Alexandria	r. 1180–1209

INDEX

AUTHOR BIOGRAPHIES

The Reverend Patrick Viscuso is a Professor of Canon Law at the Antiochian House of Studies, an Orthodox canonist, and a priest of the Greek Orthodox Archdiocese of America. His doctorate in historical theology from the Catholic University of America concentrated on Byzantine and Oriental canon law, patristic studies, and Church history. He also holds a master of divinity from Holy Cross Greek Orthodox School of Theology and a bachelor of science in foreign service from the Edmund A. Walsh School of Foreign Service, Georgetown University. He is the author of numerous scholarly articles and three books: *A Quest for Reform of the Orthodox Church* (2006), *Orthodox Canon Law: A Casebook for Study* (2007, 2011 2nd ed.), and *Sexuality, Marriage, and Celibacy in Byzantine Law: The Alphabetical Collection of Matthew Blastares* (2008). Fr. Viscuso has spoken in a number of domestic and international venues, most notably the Dumbarton Oaks Spring Symposium and the North American Patristic Society. He has been President of the Byzantine Studies Association of North America, and serves as a member of the Orthodox Delegation to the North American Orthodox-Catholic Theological Consultation.

The Reverend Sidney H. Griffith, ST, PhD, is Ordinary Professor of the Department of Semitic and Egyptian Languages and Literatures at the Catholic University of America, and a leading scholar of historical and contemporary Arabic and Syrian Christianity and Muslim-Christian encounters. He serves as co-editor of *Early Christian Texts in Translation*, a monographic series published by Peeters in Leuven,

Belgium; as associate editor of the *Journal of Early Christian Studies*; as consulting editor of *Islam and Christian-Muslim Relations*; and as a member of the editorial boards of *Medieval Encounters: Jewish, Christian, and Muslim Culture in Confluence and Dialogue* and the *Bulletin of the Royal Institute for Inter-Faith Studies*. Rev. Dr. Griffith has published widely in his field and is an editor of *The Blackwell Dictionary of Early Christianity* (1999). His most recently published books are *The Church in the Shadow of the Mosque: Christians and Muslims in the World of Islam* (2008) and *The Bible in Arabic: The Scriptures of the People of the Book in the Language of the Qur'an* (2013). Rev. Dr. Griffith has been a fellow at the Institute for Advanced Studies, the Hebrew University of Jerusalem, as well as at the Dumbarton Oaks Center for Byzantine Studies. He has been president of both the Byzantine Studies Conference and the North American Patristic Society, and serves as a member of the Catholic Delegation to the North American Orthodox-Catholic Theological Consultation.

CPSIA information can be obtained
at www.ICGtesting.com
Printed in the USA
FFOW04n2324180115
10305FF

9 781935 317463